Community College Orientation

Everything begins with you

Anthony Raptis

Successmakers Publishing
P. O. Box 913
Malibu, California 90265 USA
Phone 310 230-3664
Fax 310 573-0148

E-mail SmakersPub@aol.com

Printed in Hong Kong

ISBN 0-9649018-7-0

Acknowledgements

The are many individuals who have made a significant contribution to this book. I want
to recognize Nikki Cayanan, Jo-Ann Wolfe, Johanna Dearinger, and John Dearinger for
preparation and layout of the text. Several of my colleagues made contributions to the content
of text: David Magallanes, mathematics questions, Harmony Rodriguez and Tom Stough for
web site and library questions, Dr. Emma Waits and Carmen Guerrero for review of text.
Dr. Gary Morgan for advisement and editing. A special acknowledgement to Rudy Gardea for
the inspired art design. Finally, recognition of Diana Osborne for extensive assistance with
ideas, editing, organization, and design of text.

Foreword

The *Community College Orientation* text is a framework for community college orientation and success. The text is a multi-faceted book designed to assist the student through what can seem like a maze of community college education. It will help the student get organized, develop an academic plan, check progress, reach goals, and fulfill potential. The *Community College Orientation* text is a planner, organizer, progress checker, monitor, time manager, success motivator, self-esteem builder, and skills developer.

Community College Orientation is organized into a sequence of events encountered by community college students. The text starts with enrollment procedures and continues with academic planning issues, student services, academic policies, and ends with a framework for college survival and success. The chapters include:

Starting at the Community College
Developing a Comprehensive Educational Plan
Connecting with Student Services
Conceptualizing Success
Surviving at the Community College
Managing Life Issues
Creating a Vision for the Future

The primary goal of *Community College Orientation* is to promote and enhance student success and retention through the seven steps to success which constitute the organization and foundation of the text. Each chapter in the *Community College Orientation* book represents a step to success:

Starting
Planning
Connecting
Conceptualizing
Surviving
Managing
Creating

iii

Community College Orientation is designed for community college students attending community college anywhere in the United States. It is designed to help the student who has recently graduated from high school, the student who is re-entering college after an absence, and for adults entering college for the first time. The text focuses on the commonality of issues confronted by all community college students.

The *Community College Orientation* text may be used in college orientation sessions, orientation courses, student success classes, TRIO programs, and other student success courses. Students need to know how to start their college experience, plan their education, connect with available services, conceptualize success, survive at the college, manage life issues, and create a future. The instructors may assist students in starting, planning, connecting, conceptualizing, surviving, managing, and creating their life and college experience. Connecting students to relevant information is essential to their progress, success, and retention.

The *Community College Orientation* text will facilitate the counseling process. Students will quickly learn the functions and structure of the community college and will come better prepared for advising sessions. The *Community College Orientation* text will augment your students' information system.

One major objective of the *Community College Orientation* text is to present information in interesting and stimulating formats and displays. The text provides manageable information through the question-and-answer format, summary sheets, worksheets, educational planning forms, organizers, and lists of important computer sites and references. The question-and-answer format is based on the most frequently asked questions by community college students. The questions are grouped into related topics which facilitate the use of the *Community College Orientation* text. The questions also reflect the experience of community college students enabling the new student to connect with useful information.

The *Community College Orientation* text is a guide which enables students to participate more effectively in planning their orientation. Students will maintain and complete an educational plan along with the opportunity to evaluate progress towards goals. Expectations will be made clear to the students. They will understand their options and make choices which will maximize their potential.

The *Community College Orientation* text prepares students for class attendance and performance, appropriate course placement, counseling sessions, career and academic planning, selection of appropriate goals and degrees, choice of major, and self-confidence and motivation. It is through information that students become aware of options, select goals, and achieve success. Going to college is an adventure, a journey, and a time of enthusiasm and excitement. The *Community College Orientation* text symbolizes this journey through graphic representations of travel.

There are many ways to get there.

Disclaimer

Academic information may change very rapidly. Therefore, any significant academic decision should be made with careful consultation with your counselor or advisor. We cannot guarantee that all information in *Community College Orientation* is applicable and accurate for you. Following the academic planning process contained in this text should help mitigate any significant academic planning error.

Welcome to Your Community College

Congratulations! You are taking a step forward to further the quality of your life. You have made an excellent choice to achieve your life goals. You are exercising one of your best options to advance yourself. The community college provides many valuable learning opportunities.

Today's world requires advanced training in new technologies, knowledge of the communication revolution and major advances in biotechnology, and the ability to compete in a global economy and cope with a rapidly changing world.

Your community college provides instruction at a reasonable cost. While tuition costs rise significantly at four-year colleges and universities, tuition at community colleges has seen comparatively moderate increases. As you enter your community college, you are not confronted with restrictive admission requirements. Your community college is a convenient and accessible place to pursue your educational goals.

Your community college is a friendly and enjoyable place to be. You will find many individuals who share common interests and have similar goals. You can enlarge your world at the community college by meeting students of different backgrounds, but with whom you have a lot in common. You can actualize your potential. You learn to read and write at a higher level, improve your math skills, and develop important social skills. You can expand your world by attending a community college.

Table of Contents

Chapter 2   Developing Your Educational Plan   61

Chapter 3   Connecting with Student Services   91

Chapter 4   Conceptualizing Success   105

Chapter 5   Surviving at the Community College   121

Community College Orientation

The *Community College Orientation* text is a general orientation and college success book for all community college students. Wherever you attend community college, you will encounter comparable issues and share the same concerns as other students in community colleges throughout the country. Community colleges have similar structures, operations, procedures and policies, programs, degrees, and missions. However, community colleges are unique and can be significantly different in many respects. Throughout this book, be sure to identify what specifically applies to you.

The *Community College Orientation* book is designed to help you:

Become aware of your options

Understand the structure, operations, policies and procedures of your community college

Learn academic requirements

Maximize your potential

Engage in effective planning

Study and learn effectively

Make a career choice

The *Community College Orientation* book recognizes you among the following:

An adult learner

Working and going to school

Working full-time and going to school

From a disadvantaged background

First in family to go to college

Had no college prep in high school

Had some college prep in high school

Head of household

A single parent

A recent high school graduate

A re-entry student

The *Community College Orientation* book places the emphasis on *you* as a community college student.

Why and When?

Why use this book?

To focus on you, the community college student

To give you a comprehensive orientation to your community college

To help you understand the value of your community college education

To help you discover your purpose in being at the community college

To help you establish direction in you life

To help you know your options at the community college

To help you learn and access information

To help you maximize your potential

When you use this book you will:

Learn from the general to the specific

Separate out what is relevant to you

Memorize facts

Develop a comprehensive educational plan

Respond to all questions and complete all activities

Apply concepts to everyday life

Read for information

Everything Begins with You

"Everything begins with you" means that whatever you accomplish at the community college is your responsibility, and it is up to you to choose wisely from a wide range of options. Self-responsibility is central to success at the community college. You have many learning activities to complete, some of which require careful self-examination. Knowing yourself is the foundation for developing direction in college and life and fundamental to educational planning. Your educational experience begins with the decisions you make.

In community college you will:

Engage in a process of self–discovery

Determine the kind of person you are

Decide what you want of life

Determine your values

Make many life–forming decisions

Determine what is best for you

Decide what you will do at the community college

Choose which degrees, options, and goals to pursue

Develop an educational plan

The Choices Are Yours

By Actively and Consciously Choosing, We Direct the Course of Our Lives

Decision-making is the navigational tool by which we set the course of our lives. The more conscious we are of our decisions, the clearer the plotting of our course. When we get off course, we can decide to get back on course or to change direction completely. When you are not conscious of your decisions, you are not the navigator of your course.

If You Don't Like Who You Are, Re-Decide Who You Are

Decision-making is a defining activity. We define who and what we are through decision-making. We can undo prior decisions we have made about ourselves. We can "re-decide" who we are. Consciously choosing ourselves is an enormously important process. Ultimately, we decide who we are. I define myself, and if I don't like my self-definition, I can re-decide who I am.

To Choose, You Must Know You Have a Choice

Many individuals do not acknowledge that choices have led them to where they are now in their lives. They did not realize that they had a choice. If you don't know you have a choice, you don't have a choice. Many individuals are so overwhelmed by their environments that they believe their lives are determined. Many of our personal problems are so confusing and frustrating that we do not realize we have a choice. Awareness of choice is essential to the decision-making process.

Our Behavior Results from Decisions

We make decisions about who we are and what we are. What we have decided about ourselves shapes our attitudes. Our attitudes determine how we think, feel, and act. We behave according to our decisions even in situations where we cannot remember making the decision. We decide what is right and wrong, what is desirable and undesirable, what is positive or negative, and what direction to pursue. We act in accordance with our decisions.

Decision-Making Skills Can Be Learned

Examining the decision-making process helps us understand how people decide. Skills such as collecting information, defining problems, generating and weighing alternatives, selecting an alternative, and implementing decisions are skills which can be learned. Decision-making involves bringing about desirable situations, conditions, circumstances, events, and personal states of satisfaction.

Freedom of Choice Is Fundamental to Decision-Making

When we view ourselves as decision-makers, we believe in our capacity to direct our own lives. A belief in the freedom to choose encourages decision-making. We cannot control all the events in our lives, but we have a significant degree of control over our lives through decision-making. If we believe that everything is determined, we may feel that we have no ability to choose.

College Essentials

College Essentials are guidelines designed to help you maximize your success at the community college. These essentials are based on observation of community college students who have enjoyed great success at the community college.

To be successful:

Start with yourself

Know your options

Don't eliminate options prematurely

Build on strengths

Overcome self-doubt

Be patient

Don't limit yourself

Focus your effort

Use time wisely

Expect good performance from yourself

Enjoy the college experience

Work hard

Student Responsibilities

You are responsible for your success. Many of your responsibilities fall into these three categories: institutional, educational planning, and classroom. An example of an institutional responsibility is knowing dates and deadlines in order to act on important administrative functions such as a deadline to withdraw from classes. An example of educational planning is knowing graduation requirements. An example of a classroom responsibility is knowing the instructor's attendance policy. Get informed about your responsibilities as a student.

Institutional Responsibilities

Student rights
Deadlines
Dates
Withdrawal from classes
Academic requirements
Services
Resources

Educational Planning Responsibilities

Graduation requirements
Major requirements
Educational plan
Transfer requirements
Maintain satisfactory Grade Point Average (GPA)

Classroom Responsibilities

Syllabus/Syllabi
Course requirements
Reading and course assignments
Instructor's attendance policy
Due dates of assignments
Attend class
Take responsibility for learning
Take notes
Do homework
Behavior
Attitude
Class participation

What to Expect

If you know what to expect at the community college, you will have an opportunity to function more effectively in the college environment. There will be no surprises. You will know what is happening and what is expected from you. You can prepare yourself. At the community college, you will be treated as an adult. Therefore, others may not necessarily watch over you or assume responsibility for your success. Students act independently and responsibly in the community college environment.

Expect the following at the community college:

Greater independence and self-responsibility

Less class time, more study time

Significant amount of reading

Major memorization tasks

Considerable number of writing assignments

Researching and information gathering

Starting
at the
Community
College

CHAPTER

1

1 What Are Community Colleges?

Community colleges are two-year colleges also known as city colleges, junior colleges, associate of arts colleges and trade and technical colleges. They are distinguished by their ability to offer fully accredited Associate of Arts or Associate of Science degrees. Community colleges also offer certificates of achievement in many occupational, vocational, and technical areas. Community colleges frequently have the capacity to respond directly to the needs of the community.

2 Who Can Attend the Community College?

Community colleges have an open access policy which allows almost anyone 18 years and older to attend. Many high school students are able to attend community college through advanced placement programs. Individuals under 18 years of age may also be able to attend community college if they already have a high school diploma, GED, and/or high school proficiency. Open enrollment provides access to almost anyone capable of profiting from a college education.

What Pathways Are Available at the Community College?

Many pathways are available to community college students. Community colleges serve the general public and provide a broad spectrum of educational options for the communities they serve. You can learn to improve your reading, writing, and math at the community college. You can learn to operate a computer. You can learn French. You can learn virtually anything that captures your interest.

Upon entering the community college, many students declare that their main educational purpose is to transfer to a four-year college or university. A substantial group of students want to pursue an occupational/technical education, and many others pursue a basic skills education. A significant number of students enter the community college to acquire job skills or to update their job skills. Others enter to re-train. Still other students want to take advantage of the life-long learning opportunities provided by the community college. Community colleges also serve their communities by offering contract education, which involves special partnerships between business and the community college to develop and train employees.

Choosing a Pathway

What does your community college have to offer you? Many pathways are available to you, and you may choose one or more of the following:

- *Associate's Degrees, Certificates of Completion, and Certificates of Achievement:* The major community college pathways are the acquisition of an associate's degree, certificates of completion, and certificates of achievement. The acquisition of any degree and/or certificate provides lifetime benefits to the student. Completion of the pathways indicates levels of proficiency, knowledge, and skills.

- *Transfer Education:* Many students choose this option. Students can complete the first two years of a four-year degree program at a community college and then transfer to a four-year college or university to complete the last two years. Most students complete the general education requirements and major requirements before transfer.

- *Occupational/Technical Education:* Community colleges offer a broad range of occupational and technical programs. You can learn computer networking, legal assisting, criminal justice, and many more specialties in occupational and technical education. You can earn degrees and certificates which certify your knowledge and skill. Many students pursue this pathway and obtain two-year degrees and certificates. Many students who choose this pathway do not transfer to a university, although some do.

- *Basic Skills Education:* The focus of this community college function is on language and math skills development. Many students need to brush up on their English and math skills, while others need more intensive instruction to get their language and math skills up to college level. Many individuals are acquiring English as their second language and need a broad-based language development program.

- *Job Skills Acquisition:* This pathway serves as a vital function for students wishing to acquire job skills and to enter the job market as soon as possible. These programs can be from short-to long-range duration, but the focus is on developing job skills. Sometimes, with the help of a counselor, you may have to formulate a unique job skills development program.

- *Update Job Skills:* Many students have already been in the job market but now need to upgrade their job skills. With advances in technology, this is becoming a major function of the community college. Continuing education and training is a major function of the community college.

- *Retraining:* Many students who have been in the job market find that their skills are now obsolete and need to retrain. Many options are available to these students including pursuing some of the pathways already described. Learning new job skills involves knowing which skills are currently in demand and the expected viability of these skills.

- *Life-Long Learning:* Learning is a life-long journey, and community colleges promote this viewpoint by providing access to students of all ages, backgrounds, races and gender. In many instances, you can be a student for as long as you want without fear of taking too long. You only need to be concerned with your academic standing and whether you are repeating prior coursework.

- *Contract Education:* Many community colleges contract with business organizations to provide training and other educational services to business employees. You can inquire at your community college to identify contract education opportunities.

Many community colleges incorporate each of these pathways into their instructional programs. Others may concentrate on one or more of these roles. Some community colleges focus exclusively on occupational and technical education. You can determine the emphasis of your community college by careful review of the college catalog. Once you review your catalog, you will realize that community colleges have a lot to offer!

5

Pathways Available at the Community College

Associate Degrees

Certificates of Achievement

Certificates of Completion

Transfer Education

Occupational/Technical Education

Basic Skills Education

Job Skills Acquisition

Update Job Skills

Retraining

Life-Long Learning

Contract Education

4 How Do I Enroll in the Community College?

Step 1 Schedule of Classes

Your first step to enroll in a community college is to obtain a Schedule of Classes for the coming semester or quarter. The Schedule of Classes booklet is usually available on campus at the college bookstore, the admissions office, the library, the counseling office, and at other locations. Many community colleges mail schedules to homes within their service area. Review the Schedule of Classes to get a perspective on the academic program of your community college. Take note of the calendar for the coming quarter or semester. Underline or highlight important phone numbers and web addresses.

Step 2 College Application

Your second step is to submit a college application which is available at the college's admissions office or online. Also, applications are frequently included in the schedule of classes. Submit the application and order transcripts from high school and other colleges.

Step 3 Placement Testing

Your third step is usually placement testing and possibly other assessment requirements. Taking the assessment is usually a requirement for enrollment. Ask for a schedule of testing times and places. Take the assessment; it's usually to your benefit. Try not to worry about your performance because the results are frequently for placement purposes only, and should not adversely affect you.

Step 4 College Orientation

Your fourth step is to attend a college orientation session. A schedule of

orientation sessions is usually available at the admissions office, the counseling office, or the testing matriculation office. This, too, may be available online. One of the benefits of in-person orientation is that a counselor may be available to help you with course selection and respond to questions and concerns you may have.

Step 5 Counseling Appointment and Selection of Classes

Your fifth step is to make a counseling appointment and to be sure the counselor has access to your assessment results. Have a tentative program sketched out and bring a list of written questions. Finalize your selection of classes for the coming semester/quarter.

Step 6 Financial Aid and Fee Waivers

The sixth step is to ask the counselor about financial aid and fee waivers for the coming quarter/semester. Do not hesitate

in applying for financial aid because it delays your first allocation of funds. Apply online for financial aid; it's quick and effective. Fee waivers may take one or two days to determine your eligibility.

Step 7 Registration

The seventh step is to get registered. You do not want to waste time because courses may close, and you may not be able to get all of the classes you want. Your college probably has at least three methods of registration: online, phone, and walk-in. Check your college Schedule of Classes for registration information. Especially important is the payment of fees. Make sure you know your options and deadlines for fee payment.

Step 7 Cost of Books

The eighth step is to determine the cost of your books. Go to the college bookstore and identify the textbooks you will be using for each of your courses and their cost.

Steps to Enroll

Step 1
Schedule of Classes

Step 2
College Application

Step 3
Placement Testing

Step 4
College Orientation

Step 5
**Counseling Appointment
and Selection of Classes**

Step 6
Financial Aid and Fee Waivers

Step 7
Registration

Step 8
Cost of Books

⑤ What Is Matriculation?

Matriculation is a process comprised of several activities designed to help the community college student achieve academic success. The components of the process include admissions and records, orientation, counseling and advisement, and follow-up. One of the major aspects of this process is the development of a student educational plan. This plan usually consists of a list of recommended courses for the first semester. Your participation in this process may be mandatory or may be strongly recommended. There are criteria which may allow you to be exempted from the matriculation process. If you complete the activities recommended in this orientation text, you will complete the matriculation process. Your community college may not appear to have a matriculation program by this name, but if you look closely at your college you will find that a different name is used for the same process.

The Matriculation Process

Admissions and Records

Orientation

Counseling and Advisement

Follow–up

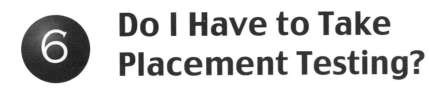

6 Do I Have to Take Placement Testing?

- Many community colleges require assessment or placement testing prior to registration. Placement testing is mandatory and is used to determine the level of courses for which you are prepared.

- At some community colleges, pursuit of a degree requires admission into a degree program. Admission is frequently based on testing. This could limit courses available for open enrollment.

- Many community colleges require completion of developmental courses prior to enrolling in baccalaureate level courses.

- Some community colleges allow for enrollment into baccalaureate level courses without testing as long as the student is not taking English or math.

- All community colleges employ a system of prerequisites for advanced level courses, and many use this system along with co-requisites. Co-requisites are courses which must be taken concurrently with other courses.

- Few community colleges require academic achievement testing such as the SAT prior to enrollment in baccalaureate level courses.

- Most community colleges have an exemption system which allows standardized testing results to be used instead of institutional testing.

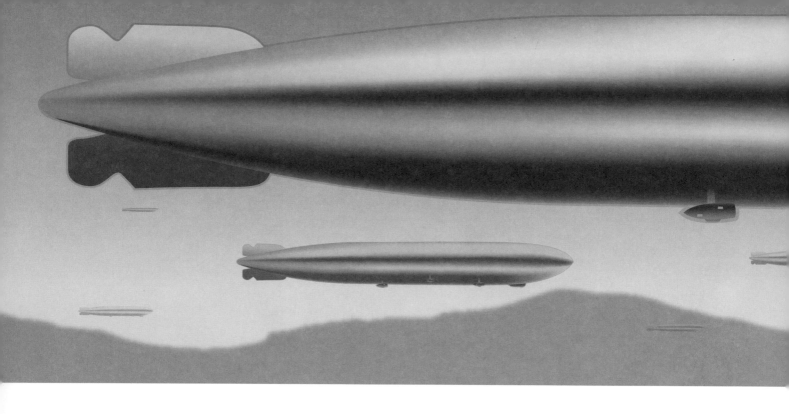

7 What Classes Should I Take?

Everything begins with you. What do you want to take? What will keep you motivated? Why are you at the community college? Which pathway seems consistent with your goals? What are your goals? Your responses to the preceding questions will provide indicators of what you should take.

When deciding on what to take, focus on interests, general education, and major requirements. What are your interests, and which requirements apply to your major and goals? Many students want to focus on general education requirements and courses required in their majors.

Re–Learning Is a Key to College Survival

You may want to choose courses you have previously studied. For example, you may have taken a general biology course in high school, and now you want to take it in college.

Re-learning subject matter previously learned is much easier than learning something completely new. You may want to study subjects in which you have some background in order to insure success. If not, you probably will have to work harder to master subjects completely new to you.

Balance Your Course Load

In selecting a course of study, you want to maximize your opportunity to succeed. You need to be especially concerned about establishing a balanced course load. You want to evaluate the weight of your course load. Is it light, medium, or heavy. You can make this determination by identifying the number of solids you are taking and the number of credits and transferable credits you are carrying. Solids include math, science, and other demanding courses. Careful selection of your course load should include a proper mix of courses. For example, in all probability, you do not want to take two science courses in the same semester. Be careful of course overload. You are better off taking less units and doing well than taking more units and doing average or worse.

Choosing Your Classes

A major consideration in planning an academic course of study is the selection of appropriate level courses. Your reading level is probably the most important factor in predicting your success at the community college. Be sure to discuss with your counselor whether your reading level is appropriate for the college level courses. The assessments and the multiple measures used by your academic advisor should be very helpful in determining your placement. You need to be especially careful in choosing English and math courses. Keep in mind that the selection of your courses is ultimately your responsibility. In selecting your courses, you want to maximize your success by doing the following:

- *Take the College Assessment:* Many community colleges offer assessments in English and math. These assessments may be very helpful in assisting you and your advisor in selecting appropriate courses for you.
- *Attend College Orientation:* The college orientation is an excellent method for familiarizing yourself with your college program and campus services. It is a time to meet the staff and your fellow students. This is an excellent place to start your initiation into college.
- *Read the College Catalog and Schedule of Classes:* These are your basic educational planning tools. They contain most of the information you will need to achieve your goals at the community college.
- *Review Graduation Requirements:* Graduation requirements are usually available on curriculum guides. Ask your counselor for a copy. Be sure to familiarize yourself with the requirements to graduate. You do not need to memorize the entire pattern, but you should have a good understanding of how you plan to fulfill the requirements.
- *Review Transfer Requirements:* Transfer information is usually available on curriculum guides and the college catalog. You may also have to use the catalog of the college to which you want to transfer.
- *Review Major Requirements:* Obtaining a curriculum guide for your major may be the easiest way to learn your major's requirements. You may use your college catalog to obtain this information.

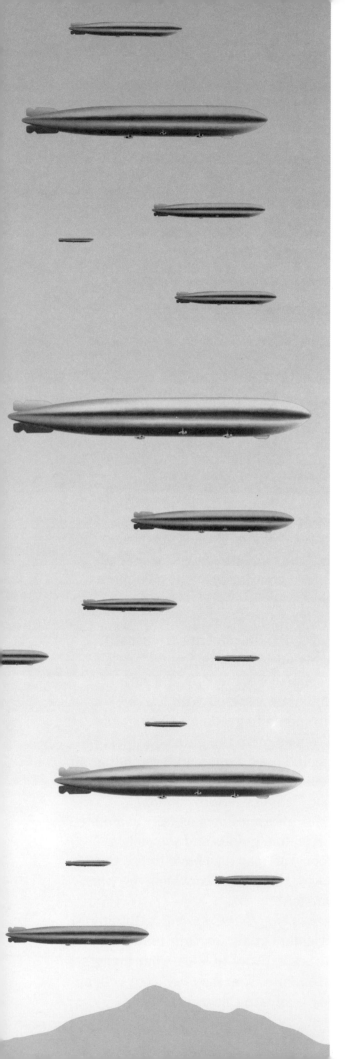

Information on transfer majors may require using the catalog of the institution where you plan to transfer.

- *Obtain a General Education Curriculum Pattern:* Most counseling programs have curriculum patterns available which help students learn what is required to earn degrees and certificates. The patterns also include guides for transfer as well as major requirements.

- *Identify Competency Requirements:* Competency requirements may or may not be applicable to your school. Some colleges, based on directives from the state, are required to maintain competency requirements. For example, you may be required to meet competency in English (reading and writing) and math.

- *Meet with an Academic Advisor:* This could be the most important step you take in developing a course of study and an education plan that will work well for you. Advisors are familiar with the college programs and they can help you with your choices.

- *Review Your High School Transcript with Your Academic Advisor:* Identifying your academic strengths and weaknesses from high school may yield important information in developing a course of study.

- *Select Courses Based on Your Interests and Strengths:*
  Selecting courses which engage your interest is an important way to start your college career. Selecting courses for which you have a background from high school may help to ensure success in college. It is important to build on your strengths and work on your weaknesses.

- *Identify Prerequisites and Co-requisites:*
  A prerequisite is a course you must complete prior to enrollment in a particular course or program. It is assumed that the student is less likely to succeed in some courses if the prerequisites are not completed first. Co-requisites represent a set of skills or body of knowledge that a student must or may acquire through concurrent enrollment in another course and without which it is doubtful the student will succeed.

To Choose Your Classes:

Take the College Assessment

Attend College Orientation

Read the College Catalog and Schedule of Classes

Review Graduation Requirements

Review Transfer Requirements

Review Major Requirements

Obtain a General Education Curriculum Pattern

Identify Competency Requirements

Meet with an Academic Advisor

Review Your High School Transcript with Your Academic Advisor

Select Courses Based on Your Interests and Strengths

Identify Prerequisites and Co-requisites

When Should I Take Classes?

8

Scheduling classes is an important issue because it may determine your success in college, and managing your time wisely is also an essential skill for student success. With this in mind, you may want to start with the fact that you have 168 hours per week to meet your needs. If you sleep 8 hours a night, that would total 56 hours a week. If you work part-time 20 hours a week, and add that to sleep hours, that would total 76 hours per week. This leaves you with 92 hours a week to complete all other life tasks. How many hours a week can you allow for your education? For many students, taking 12 credit hours (full-time) means 12 hours a week in class. If you study 3 hours for every hour in class, that would total 36 hours. Add that to 12 hours in class and the total is now 48 hours. Back to our example: add sleep hours of 56, plus work hours of 20, plus class hours of 12, plus study hours of 36, and the total is 124 hours. Subtract from the total week hours 124 from 168 and you have 44 hours left to do everything else. Time is a limited resource. Use your time wisely!

In determining your class schedule, start with the fact that you have a limited resource–time. Next, familiarize yourself with the Schedule of Classes, and develop a clear knowledge of the college program and scheduling structure. Plan a realistic class schedule through careful analysis of time availability for college commitments. Determine the number of hours per day/per week you can devote to class attendance. How many units can you take based on availability of hours? Will you attend classes five days a week, three days a week, or just one day a week? Will you construct a Monday-Wednesday-Friday schedule or a Tuesday-Thursday schedule? For many students, Monday, Wednesday, and Friday morning classes is the preferred schedule. Don't forget to allow study time between classes. For most students who work full-time, taking classes at night is their only option. Balance work schedule with family and college commitments to maximize your effectiveness without sacrificing an important area of your life.

Many community college students are doing a balancing act between work, school, and family, and they complain of not having sufficient time to do it all. How will you divide and share your time? What will you have to give up? For many individuals, it is their education. Therefore, it is essential that you examine your time use critically. You may want to use the example described earlier. Add sleep hours, work hours, family hours, class hours, study hours, and the time you need to do everything else. What kind of an academic load can you carry? How many classes can you take? When will you take them? The answers to these questions will help you get organized, allocate time, and decide what is important to you.

How Do I Construct a Class Schedule?

1

Familiarize yourself with the schedule of classes.

2

Plan a realistic schedule.

3

**Determine the number of hours per day/per week
you can devote to class attendance.**

4

**Determine how many units you can take based on avail-
ability of hours.**

5

**Will you attend classes five days a week, or can you
construct a Monday-Wednesday-Friday
or Tuesday-Thursday schedule?**

6

Allow study time between classes.

7

Consider night classes.

8

Consider your work schedule.

How to Read a Class Schedule

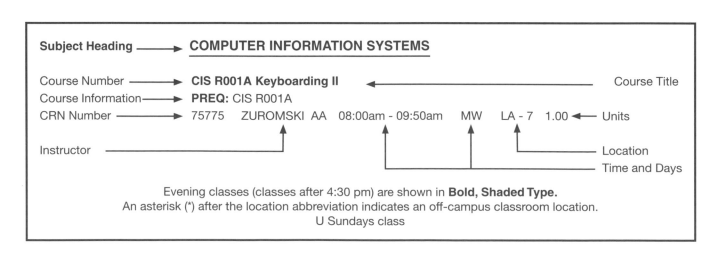

Subject Heading ——→ **COMPUTER INFORMATION SYSTEMS**

Course Number ——→ **CIS R001A Keyboarding II** ←—————————— Course Title
Course Information——→ **PREQ:** CIS R001A
CRN Number ——→ 75775   ZUROMSKI AA   08:00am - 09:50am   MW   LA - 7   1.00 ←— Units

Instructor ————————————↑   ↑   ↑   ↑————— Location
                                                                    —— Time and Days

Evening classes (classes after 4:30 pm) are shown in **Bold, Shaded Type.**
An asterisk (*) after the location abbreviation indicates an off-campus classroom location.
U Sundays class

10   What Is a Unit?

College work is measured by credit units. Sometimes college units are called credit hours. Most lecture courses using the semester structure meet three hours per week for three hours of credit. Twelve units is usually considered full time and in a lot of cases would require 12 hours of class attendance per week. Courses with a lab are different. You may have to spend more time in class than the equivalent of one unit for every hour in class. Science classes in particular may require three hours per week in lab for the equivalent of one unit of credit.

Quarter units are different from semester units. A quarter unit is worth two-thirds of a semester unit. Quarter units are used by colleges and universities on the quarter system. Quarters and semesters are of different durations. An academic year usually has two semesters or three quarters, depending on the system. The fourth quarter is usually considered summer school.

11   How Many Units Should I Take When Working?

If you work:	Take no more than:
40 hours a week	6 units
30 hours a week	9 units
20 hours a week	12 units
5-15 hours a week	14-16 units

For Veterans and Financial Aid Benefits

Take:	For:
12 units	Full Benefit
9 units	3/4 Benefit
6 units	1/2 Benefit

To be a full-time student, take at least 12 units. (See a counselor for clarification.)

For athletic eligibility in most states take at least 12 units.

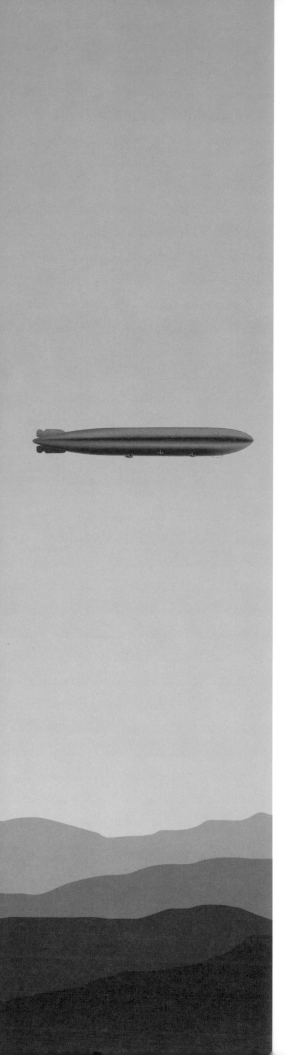

 # What Will It Cost to Attend Community College?

Your most significant expenditures excluding living expenses are enrollment and tuition fees. These fees vary greatly from state to state. Check with your community college to determine cost of attendance.

You may pay other fees such as health fees, parking fees, student body card, and any other fees which may be optional or required. An additional significant expenditure is the cost of required textbooks. Textbooks can be very expensive. You may want to purchase used books if available. Many students sell their books back at the end of the term to a textbook representative.

Living expenses are your most significant expenditure. Most important, where will you live? Most community colleges do not have dormitories. Many community college students live with their parents, rent an apartment, or have their own home, and don't forget to budget for food.

Another important expenditure is transportation. Many students have their own car while some use public transportation.

Check with your student health office to determine the availability of student health insurance. It is important to be aware of any health benefits and how to access them.

The most important step that many students take to meet the cost of college and living expenses is to apply for financial aid. Do not hesitate to apply for financial assistance. It is an important aspect of surviving and succeeding in the community college.

Student Budget

Educational Expenditures

Application Fee   _____

Tuition   _____

Health Fee   _____

Parking Fee   _____

Student Body Card   _____

Materials   _____

Books   _____

Other Fees   _____

Total =   _____

Living Expenses

Housing   _____

Transportation   _____

Food   _____

Child Care   _____

Clothing   _____

Entertainment   _____

Other   _____

Total =   _____

21

How Do I Obtain Financial Aid?

13

Many community college students rely heavily on federal and state sources for financial aid. Do not hesitate to apply. You may qualify even if you think you won't. Take advantage of the many opportunities available to you.

Financial Aid Programs

When students apply for financial aid, they are considered for the following federal, state, and private financial aid programs:

- Pell Grant
- Supplemental Educational Opportunity Grant
- Tuition Waiver
- College Work-Study Program
- Stafford Loans
- Scholarships

Eligibility

Applicants for financial aid must meet eligibility requirements in order to qualify for federal financial aid. Many states use the Free Application for Federal Aid, or FAFSA, as the instrument for qualifying students for state financial aid.

Each recipient must meet the following eligibility requirements:

- Be a U.S. citizen or an eligible non-citizen
- Have a high school diploma or GED certificate
- Be enrolled in a college degree or certificate program
- Be registered with Selective Service (if required)
- Have financial need as determined by the federal need analysis (except for unsubsidized federal Stafford loans)

How to apply

The FAFSA is used to apply for federal student aid including grants, loans, and work study.

- Complete the FAFSA
- Submit the FAFSA
- Receive the Student Aid Report (SAR)
- Receive your assistance

How to qualify

The Expected Family Contribution (EFC) is included in the Student Aid Report (SAR), which is used to determine eligibility for federal student aid, and to prepare a financial aid package to help you meet your financial need.

Financial need is the difference between your EFC and your school's cost of attendance (which can include living expenses), as determined by the school.

Any financial aid you are eligible to receive will be paid to you through your school. This process will take approximately four weeks depending on whether you go online or mail your application.

Online: www.fafsa.ed.gov
Or call: 1-800-433-3243

Academic Requirements

There are student academic performance and completion requirements to maintain eligibility for financial aid. Federal and state financial aid regulations require all recipients to maintain satisfactory academic progress in their program of study. Satisfactory progress for full-time students is completing a minimum of 12 credits each quarter/semester and maintaining a minimum of 2.0 cumulative Grade Point Average.

How Do I Use the Internet to Apply for Financial Aid?

The Internet is a convenient way to apply for financial aid. You'll get your results 7 to 14 days faster if you use the Internet instead of mailing in a paper application. Plus, because your answers are edited automatically, you'll make fewer mistakes and your school will be able to tell you sooner if you qualify for aid.

Your data are completely secure. Sending an application over the Internet is just as safe as mailing a paper form.

You're only asked the questions you need to answer because FAFSA on the Web automatically skips questions that don't apply to you. Extensive online help is available, providing you with more instructions than are found on the paper application.

What is FAFSA on the Web?

The online version of the Free Application for Federal Student Aid (FAFSA) lets you apply for student financial aid using the Internet. Schools use your FAFSA information to determine if you're eligible to receive money from federal grant, loan, and work-study programs.

In many cases, FAFSA on the Web also may be used to apply for financial aid from other sources, such as your state or school. For more information, check with your guidance counselor or college financial aid office.

Before You Begin

Gather documents showing your finances, and if you're a dependent, your parents' finances:

1. Federal income tax returns
2. W-2 forms
3. Records of untaxed benefits received
4. Current bank statements
5. Records of other savings and investments, such as stocks, bonds, and mutual funds

How to Use FAFSA on the Web

1 Open your browser and go to *www.fafsa.ed.gov*
2. Select *Entering a FAFSA*, then follow the on-screen instructions to fill out the application.
3. Review your answers and, if necessary, correct them before transmitting your application.
4. Sign your completed FAFSA. Signatures from both you and one of your parents (if you're a dependent) must be provided before your FAFSA can be processed. You have three options for signing. You can:
   - Use your PIN to electronically sign your FAFSA.
   - Print a paper signature page from FAFSA on the Web, sign it, and mail it to the address provided.
   - Transmit your online FAFSA without signing. (If you choose this option, you will receive a Student Aid Report (SAR) in the mail requesting signatures. Sign and return your SAR to continue processing.)
5. Submit your application. When you have completed your FAFSA, click on "Submit my application now." Your application will be transmitted over the Internet. Then, you'll be taken to a screen that says "Your application has been submitted." Note your confirmation number and your Expected Family Contribution (EFC). Your EFC is the estimated amount your family will pay for your educational expenses for one academic year.
6. You should receive your SAR in the mail about two weeks after transmitting your FAFSA over the Internet. The SAR provides information about your application and tells you what to do next. The schools listed on your online FAFSA will get electronic copies of your SAR so that they can figure out how much federal financial aid you can receive.

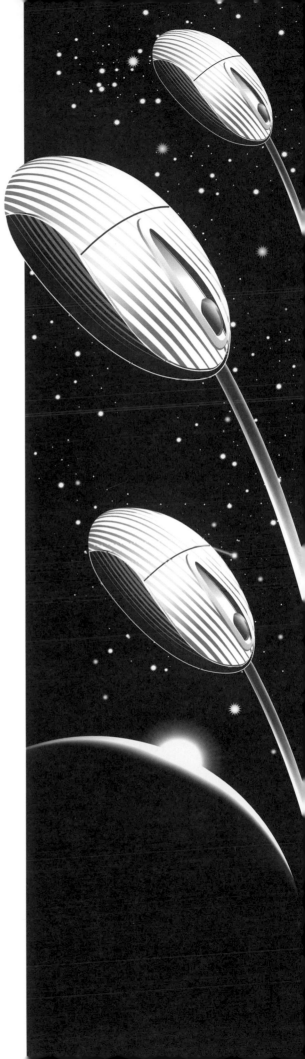

15 What Websites Can I Use to Find Financial Aid, Scholarships, and Grants?

You can find financial aid information on the world wide web. Check regularly to make sure they remain live links.

www.fastWeb.com

www.srnexpress.com

www.fie.com/molis/scholar.htm

www.aynrand.org/contests

www.finaid.org

www.collegeboard.org/fundfinder/html/

www.collegequest.com/cgi-bin/ndCGI/collegeQuest/pgGateway

www.gmsp.org

www.hispanicfund.org

www.chci.org

www.hacu.net

www.el-dorado.ca.us/-grants/seekers.shtml

www.firn.edu/doe

www.scholaraid.com

www.collegelink.com

16 What Other College and Financial Aid Information Is Available?

College and University Guides

College & Career Programs for Deaf Students	REF HV2510 .C64
The College Blue Book: Narrative Descriptions	REF LA226.C685 v.1
The Multicultural Student's Guide to Colleges	REF L901.M58
Peterson's Colleges with Programs for Students with Learning Disabilities	REF L901.P458

Financial Aid

The College Blue Book: Scholarships, Fellowships, Grants, Loans	REF LA226.C685 v.5
Directory of Financial Aid for Women	REF LB2338.D564
Financial Aid for African Americans	REF LB2338.F5643
Financial Aid for Asian Americans	REF LB2338.F5644
Financial Aid for Hispanic Americans	REF LB2338.F5645
Financial Aid for Native Americans	REF LB2338.F5646

The Admissions Process

Choosing a College: A Guide for Parents and Students	LB2350.5 .S64
College Applications and Essays	REF LB2351.52.U6 V37
Write Your Way into College: A Successful Application Essay	LB2351.5.E37

Web Sites

California Student Aid Commission	http://www.csac.ca.gov/default.asp
College Board.com	http://www.collegeboard.org
Federal Student Aid	http://www.fafsa.ed.gov/
Financial Aid & Tests Preparation	http://iiswinprd03.petersons.com/finaid/
Guide to Financial Aid	http://www.finaid.org
Information for the Re-Entry Student	http://www.back2college.com/
U.S. Dept. of Education	http://www.ed.gov/index.jsp

 # How Can I Manage My Time?

One of the best ways to get things done is to manage time effectively. The purpose of time management is to get things done in order to accomplish goals. Time management is concerned with managing the present in order to manage the future.

Managing your time has many benefits. The most important benefit is the necessity to examine your life. Are you achieving the things you want to accomplish? Are you getting what you want out of life? Are you meeting your commitments? Are you spending time doing the things that matter most? These questions are related to your level of happiness and satisfaction in life. Time management aims to make you more productive by showing you how to use time more effectively. Time management structures your life, and most of us function better when our lives are well structured. Time management allows you to know how you actually spend your time. As a consequence, you feel better about yourself because you know when you are being productive and when time is being wasted. Above all, you feel better about yourself because you have taken control of your life.

Time management is similar to a weight reduction program. Both require a high level of motivation, a present status assessment, monitoring, accurate and consistent record keeping, gradual change, and an assessment of progress. Time management requires a commitment because you will have to examine goals, priorities, values, make daily "to do" lists, review what you are doing and not doing, and you will have to make a real effort to change.

18 How Can I Develop a Time Schedule?

Start by **assessing** your motivation to maintain a time schedule. A commitment to maintaining a time schedule will facilitate your time schedule development and utilization. **Monitoring** your time use is an important step in seeing how you actually spend your time and is an important preliminary step in the schedule developing process. Time monitoring gives you an overview of how you use your time and requires that you look closely at what you are doing. When you monitor your time, **record** how you spend twenty-four hours a day during a one week period. Monitoring your activities will give you valuable insight into how you use your time. The time monitor sheet consists of a 24-hour schedule divided into one hour increments. Each hour is divided by a center line that allows your to write in time use for the first and second half hour. Record your activities for each half hour. After you have monitored your time for seven days, review your time monitor sheets and evaluate them. Look at your activity totals at the bottom of each page. Calculate totals for the week and determine your major time users. You should be able to determine with some precision the amount of time you spend on each activity.

At the end of the seven day monitoring period, **construct** a tentative time schedule. **Begin** with committed times such as class, work, and travel times. Live with this schedule for a short period. Are your comfortable with this schedule? Are you getting things done? What insights have you derived from monitoring your time? Are you aware of how you use your time? As you live with this schedule **evaluate** your time utilization. Can you identify half hour increments that you consider wasted time? If you can identify wasted time, **change** unproductive time periods into productive time periods. If you are not successful at maintaining a time schedule, **re-evaluate** your motivation to maintain a time schedule. Maintaining a time schedule is helpful, not obligatory. If you feel compelled or coerced into maintaining a time schedule, you are less likely to keep a useful time schedule. A time schedule is not a promise to go far beyond the way you customarily use your time. The way you use your time is habitual. Most of us cannot easily change our habits. Therefore, plan to change your time utilization gradually.

Daily Time Monitor

Day/Date:_____

6:00 a.m.	_____	6:30 a.m.
7:00 a.m.	_____	7:30 a.m.
8:00 a.m.	_____	8:30 a.m.
9:00 a.m.	_____	9:30 a.m.
10:00 a.m.	_____	10:30 a.m.
11:00 a.m.	_____	11:30 a.m.
12:00 p.m.	_____	12:30 p.m.
1:00 p.m.	_____	1:30 p.m.
2:00 p.m.	_____	2:30 p.m.
3:00 p.m.	_____	3:30 p.m.
4:00 p.m.	_____	4:30 p.m.
5:00 p.m.	_____	5:30 p.m.
6:00 p.m.	_____	6:30 p.m.
7:00 p.m.	_____	7:30 p.m.
8:00 p.m.	_____	8:30 p.m.
9:00 p.m.	_____	9:30 p.m.
10:00 p.m.	_____	10:30 p.m.
11:00 p.m.	_____	11:30 p.m.
12:00 a.m.	_____	12:30 a.m.
1:00 a.m.	_____	1:30 a.m.
2:00 a.m.	_____	2:30 a.m.
3:00 a.m.	_____	3:30 a.m.
4:00 a.m.	_____	4:30 a.m.
5:00 a.m.	_____	5:30 a.m.
6:00 a.m.	_____	6:30 a.m.

Categories	Hours Spent	Categories	Hours Spent	Categories	Hours Spent
Work		Study		Social	
Sleep		Family		TV	
Eating		Commuting		Errands	
Grooming		Cooking		Housekeeping	
Class		Exercise			

Daily Time Monitor

Day/Date:_____

6:00 a.m.	6:30 a.m.
7:00 a.m.	7:30 a.m.
8:00 a.m.	8:30 a.m.
9:00 a.m.	9:30 a.m.
10:00 a.m.	10:30 a.m.
11:00 a.m.	11:30 a.m.
12:00 p.m.	12:30 p.m.
1:00 p.m.	1:30 p.m.
2:00 p.m.	2:30 p.m.
3:00 p.m.	3:30 p.m.
4:00 p.m.	4:30 p.m.
5:00 p.m.	5:30 p.m.
6:00 p.m.	6:30 p.m.
7:00 p.m.	7:30 p.m.
8:00 p.m.	8:30 p.m.
9:00 p.m.	9:30 p.m.
10:00 p.m.	10:30 p.m.
11:00 p.m.	11:30 p.m.
12:00 a.m.	12:30 a.m.
1:00 a.m.	1:30 a.m.
2:00 a.m.	2:30 a.m.
3:00 a.m.	3:30 a.m.
4:00 a.m.	4:30 a.m.
5:00 a.m.	5:30 a.m.
6:00 a.m.	6:30 a.m.

Categories	Hours Spent	Categories	Hours Spent	Categories	Hours Spent
Work		Study		Social	
Sleep		Family		TV	
Eating		Commuting		Errands	
Grooming		Cooking		Housekeeping	
Class		Exercise			

31

Daily Time Monitor

Day/Date:_____

6:00 a.m.	6:30 a.m.
7:00 a.m.	7:30 a.m.
8:00 a.m.	8:30 a.m.
9:00 a.m.	9:30 a.m.
10:00 a.m.	10:30 a.m.
11:00 a.m.	11:30 a.m.
12:00 p.m.	12:30 p.m.
1:00 p.m.	1:30 p.m.
2:00 p.m.	2:30 p.m.
3:00 p.m.	3:30 p.m.
4:00 p.m.	4:30 p.m.
5:00 p.m.	5:30 p.m.
6:00 p.m.	6:30 p.m.
7:00 p.m.	7:30 p.m.
8:00 p.m.	8:30 p.m.
9:00 p.m.	9:30 p.m.
10:00 p.m.	10:30 p.m.
11:00 p.m.	11:30 p.m.
12:00 a.m.	12:30 a.m.
1:00 a.m.	1:30 a.m.
2:00 a.m.	2:30 a.m.
3:00 a.m.	3:30 a.m.
4:00 a.m.	4:30 a.m.
5:00 a.m.	5:30 a.m.
6:00 a.m.	6:30 a.m.

Categories	Hours Spent	Categories	Hours Spent	Categories	Hours Spent
Work		Study		Social	
Sleep		Family		TV	
Eating		Commuting		Errands	
Grooming		Cooking		Housekeeping	
Class		Exercise			

Daily Time Monitor

Day/Date:_____

6:00 a.m. _____	6:30 a.m.
7:00 a.m. _____	7:30 a.m.
8:00 a.m. _____	8:30 a.m.
9:00 a.m. _____	9:30 a.m.
10:00 a.m. _____	10:30 a.m.
11:00 a.m. _____	11:30 a.m.
12:00 p.m. _____	12:30 p.m.
1:00 p.m. _____	1:30 p.m.
2:00 p.m. _____	2:30 p.m.
3:00 p.m. _____	3:30 p.m.
4:00 p.m. _____	4:30 p.m.
5:00 p.m. _____	5:30 p.m.
6:00 p.m. _____	6:30 p.m.
7:00 p.m. _____	7:30 p.m.
8:00 p.m. _____	8:30 p.m.
9:00 p.m. _____	9:30 p.m.
10:00 p.m. _____	10:30 p.m.
11:00 p.m. _____	11:30 p.m.
12:00 a.m. _____	12:30 a.m.
1:00 a.m. _____	1:30 a.m.
2:00 a.m. _____	2:30 a.m.
3:00 a.m. _____	3:30 a.m.
4:00 a.m. _____	4:30 a.m.
5:00 a.m. _____	5:30 a.m.
6:00 a.m. _____	6:30 a.m.

Categories	Hours Spent
Work	
Sleep	
Eating	
Grooming	
Class	

Categories	Hours Spent
Study	
Family	
Commuting	
Cooking	
Exercise	

Categories	Hours Spent
Social	
TV	
Errands	
Housekeeping	

Daily Time Monitor

Day/Date:_____

6:00 a.m.	6:30 a.m.
7:00 a.m.	7:30 a.m.
8:00 a.m.	8:30 a.m.
9:00 a.m.	9:30 a.m.
10:00 a.m.	10:30 a.m.
11:00 a.m.	11:30 a.m.
12:00 p.m.	12:30 p.m.
1:00 p.m.	1:30 p.m.
2:00 p.m.	2:30 p.m.
3:00 p.m.	3:30 p.m.
4:00 p.m.	4:30 p.m.
5:00 p.m.	5:30 p.m.
6:00 p.m.	6:30 p.m.
7:00 p.m.	7:30 p.m.
8:00 p.m.	8:30 p.m.
9:00 p.m.	9:30 p.m.
10:00 p.m.	10:30 p.m.
11:00 p.m.	11:30 p.m.
12:00 a.m.	12:30 a.m.
1:00 a.m.	1:30 a.m.
2:00 a.m.	2:30 a.m.
3:00 a.m.	3:30 a.m.
4:00 a.m.	4:30 a.m.
5:00 a.m.	5:30 a.m.
6:00 a.m.	6:30 a.m.

Categories	Hours Spent	Categories	Hours Spent	Categories	Hours Spent
Work		Study		Social	
Sleep		Family		TV	
Eating		Commuting		Errands	
Grooming		Cooking		Housekeeping	
Class		Exercise			

34

Daily Time Monitor

Day/Date:_____

6:00 a.m.	6:30 a.m.
7:00 a.m.	7:30 a.m.
8:00 a.m.	8:30 a.m.
9:00 a.m.	9:30 a.m.
10:00 a.m.	10:30 a.m.
11:00 a.m.	11:30 a.m.
12:00 p.m.	12:30 p.m.
1:00 p.m.	1:30 p.m.
2:00 p.m.	2:30 p.m.
3:00 p.m.	3:30 p.m.
4:00 p.m.	4:30 p.m.
5:00 p.m.	5:30 p.m.
6:00 p.m.	6:30 p.m.
7:00 p.m.	7:30 p.m.
8:00 p.m.	8:30 p.m.
9:00 p.m.	9:30 p.m.
10:00 p.m.	10:30 p.m.
11:00 p.m.	11:30 p.m.
12:00 a.m.	12:30 a.m.
1:00 a.m.	1:30 a.m.
2:00 a.m.	2:30 a.m.
3:00 a.m.	3:30 a.m.
4:00 a.m.	4:30 a.m.
5:00 a.m.	5:30 a.m.
6:00 a.m.	6:30 a.m.

Categories	Hours Spent	Categories	Hours Spent	Categories	Hours Spent
Work		Study		Social	
Sleep		Family		TV	
Eating		Commuting		Errands	
Grooming		Cooking		Housekeeping	
Class		Exercise			

Daily Time Monitor

Day/Date:_____

6:00 a.m.	6:30 a.m.
7:00 a.m.	7:30 a.m.
8:00 a.m.	8:30 a.m.
9:00 a.m.	9:30 a.m.
10:00 a.m.	10:30 a.m.
11:00 a.m.	11:30 a.m.
12:00 p.m.	12:30 p.m.
1:00 p.m.	1:30 p.m.
2:00 p.m.	2:30 p.m.
3:00 p.m.	3:30 p.m.
4:00 p.m.	4:30 p.m.
5:00 p.m.	5:30 p.m.
6:00 p.m.	6:30 p.m.
7:00 p.m.	7:30 p.m.
8:00 p.m.	8:30 p.m.
9:00 p.m.	9:30 p.m.
10:00 p.m.	10:30 p.m.
11:00 p.m.	11:30 p.m.
12:00 a.m.	12:30 a.m.
1:00 a.m.	1:30 a.m.
2:00 a.m.	2:30 a.m.
3:00 a.m.	3:30 a.m.
4:00 a.m.	4:30 a.m.
5:00 a.m.	5:30 a.m.
6:00 a.m.	6:30 a.m.

Categories	Hours Spent
Work	
Sleep	
Eating	
Grooming	
Class	

Categories	Hours Spent
Study	
Family	
Commuting	
Cooking	
Exercise	

Categories	Hours Spent
Social	
TV	
Errands	
Housekeeping	

Weekly Time Schedule

	Monday	Tuesday	Wednesday	Thursday	Friday
6:00 a.m.					
7:00 a.m.					
8:00 a.m.					
9:00 a.m.					
10:00 a.m.					
11:00 a.m.					
12:00 p.m.					
1:00 p.m.					
2:00 p.m.					
3:00 p.m.					
4:00 p.m.					
5:00 p.m.					
6:00 p.m.					
7:00 p.m.					
8:00 p.m.					
9:00 p.m.					
10:00 p.m.					
11:00 p.m.					
12:00 a.m.					
1:00 a.m.					
2:00 a.m.					
3:00 a.m.					
4:00 a.m.					
5:00 a.m.					
6:00 a.m.					

	Saturday	**Sunday**
6:00 a.m.		
7:00 a.m.		
8:00 a.m.		
9:00 a.m.		
10:00 a.m.		
11:00 a.m.		
12:00 p.m.		
1:00 p.m.		
2:00 p.m.		
3:00 p.m.		
4:00 p.m.		
5:00 p.m.		
6:00 p.m.		
7:00 p.m.		
8:00 p.m.		
9:00 p.m.		
10:00 p.m.		
11:00 p.m.		
12:00 a.m.		
1:00 a.m.		
2:00 a.m.		
3:00 a.m.		
4:00 a.m.		
5:00 a.m.		
6:00 a.m.		

Important dates to remember

January	February	March
April	May	June
July	August	September
October	November	December

Assignment/Test Calendar

SEM/QTR   Month

MONDAY	TUESDAY	WEDNESDAY	THURSDAY	FRIDAY

Assignment/Test Calendar

SEM/QTR   **Month**

MONDAY	TUESDAY	WEDNESDAY	THURSDAY	FRIDAY

Assignment/Test Calendar

MONDAY	TUESDAY	WEDNESDAY	THURSDAY	FRIDAY

Assignment/Test Calendar

SEM/QTR

Month

MONDAY	TUESDAY	WEDNESDAY	THURSDAY	FRIDAY

Assignment/Test Calendar

Month

MONDAY	TUESDAY	WEDNESDAY	THURSDAY	FRIDAY

Assignment/Test Calendar

Month

MONDAY	TUESDAY	WEDNESDAY	THURSDAY	FRIDAY

Assignment/Test Calendar

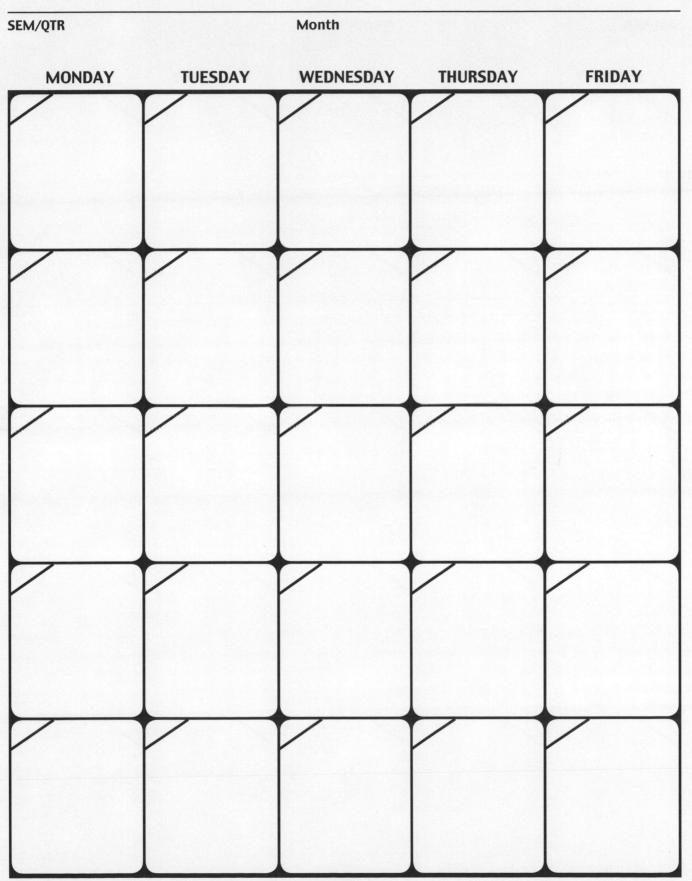

Assignment/Test Calendar

SEM/QTR   **Month**

MONDAY	TUESDAY	WEDNESDAY	THURSDAY	FRIDAY

Assignment/Test Calendar

SEM/QTR   **Month**

MONDAY	TUESDAY	WEDNESDAY	THURSDAY	FRIDAY

Assignment/Test Calendar

SEM/QTR   **Month**

MONDAY	TUESDAY	WEDNESDAY	THURSDAY	FRIDAY

Assignment/Test Calendar

MONDAY	TUESDAY	WEDNESDAY	THURSDAY	FRIDAY

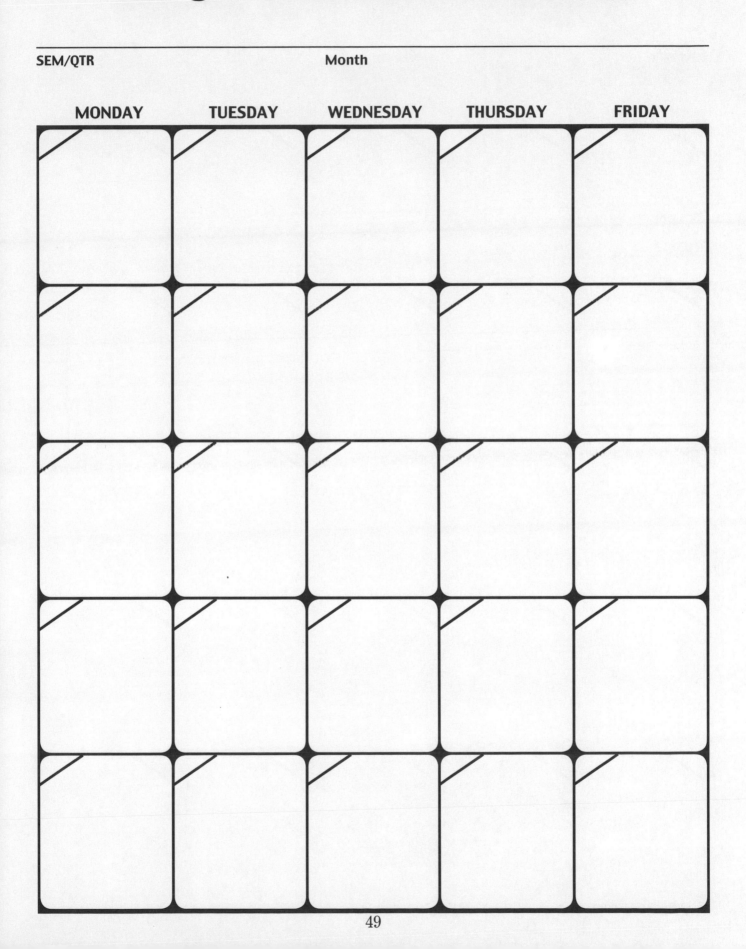

Assignment/Test Calendar

SEM/QTR   **Month**

MONDAY	TUESDAY	WEDNESDAY	THURSDAY	FRIDAY

Progress Record
Assignments/Tests and Grades

Sem/Qtr:

	Date:	Subject	Assignment/Test	Due Date	Test Date	Grade
1						
2						
3						
4						
5						
6						
7						
8						
9						
10						
11						
12						
13						
14						
15						
16						
17						
18						
19						
20						
21						
22						
23						
24						
25						
26						
27						
28						
29						
30						
31						
32						
33						

Progress Record
Assignments/Tests and Grades

Sem/Qtr:

	Date:	Subject	Assignment/Test	Due Date	Test Date	Grade
1						
2						
3						
4						
5						
6						
7						
8						
9						
10						
11						
12						
13						
14						
15						
16						
17						
18						
19						
20						
21						
22						
23						
24						
25						
26						
27						
28						
29						
30						
31						
32						
33						

Progress Record

Assignments/Tests and Grades

Sem/Qtr:

	Date:	Subject	Assignment/Test	Due Date	Test Date	Grade
1						
2						
3						
4						
5						
6						
7						
8						
9						
10						
11						
12						
13						
14						
15						
16						
17						
18						
19						
20						
21						
22						
23						
24						
25						
26						
27						
28						
29						
30						
31						
32						
33						

Progress Record
Assignments/Tests and Grades

Sem/Qtr:

	Date:	Subject	Assignment/Test	Due Date	Test Date	Grade
1						
2						
3						
4						
5						
6						
7						
8						
9						
10						
11						
12						
13						
14						
15						
16						
17						
18						
19						
20						
21						
22						
23						
24						
25						
26						
27						
28						
29						
30						
31						
32						
33						

19 How Can I Stop Wasting Time?

Do you spend a lot of time worrying about not getting things done? Do you write term papers and prepare for exams at the last moment? The key to getting things done is breaking them down into manageable tasks and activities. Set goals. What tasks and activities must you complete to get to your goals? The following approaches to using your time more effectively may help you become better organized, goal-directed, and more productive.

Time Planners

Planners come in many different formats. Go to an office supply store and look at several. Identify a planner that would work best for you. Some planners incorporate week-at-a-glance or month-at-a-glance formats, and electronic planners may be the type you would use most effectively.

Goals

Set goals by identifying what you want. Formulate goal statements based on the things you want to accomplish. State your goals in desired outcomes. Set time lines to accomplish your goals.

Priorities

Identify the activities which are most important and lead to your goals. Rank the activities in order of importance and set time lines to bring the activity to completion.

"To Do" Lists

Make daily "to do" lists. These lists will get you organized. Know what activities to complete each day that lead to your goals. Review "to do" list at end of day. Identify what was accomplished.

Create a Personal Schedule

A schedule should be based on careful time monitoring. A schedule should reflect actual time use. Unrealistic schedules are of little value. Monitor and evaluate your time use and then make a schedule.

Put Things Away

A great deal of time is wasted trying to find materials not put away into a well organized system. Where do you place term papers, returned exams, and returned assignments?

Write Down Appointments and Commitments

Write down appointments immediately. Be sure to record times and dates and make sure you do not have scheduling conflicts. Record keeping is a major task of maintaining an effective schedule.

Use "Now" To Get Things Done

You only have "now." You function "now." How are you using your "nows?" Get things done "now" before your next "now" arrives.

Productivity Rhythm

When are you most productive? Are you a morning person or a night person? Identify your productive times of the day and make sure you are making the most of your time rhythm.

Visualize Your Day

How are you going to complete each task designated for that day? Visualize how you are going to complete each task for the day and what you need to complete your daily activities. Visualize yourself finishing each task and feeling very satisfied that you have completed your work.

Complete Priorities First

Remind yourself to stay focused on completing priorities. Review priorities and see if any modifications are needed.

Use Multi–Tasking Techniques

Do more than one thing at a time if it does not decrease efficiency. Listen to a foreign language tape while you drive. This is an excellent way to support learning a foreign language.

Stay On Task

Increase your capacity to stay on task. Are you able to stay on task to completion? Do you allow many tasks to go unfinished? Are you able to concentrate for long periods of time?

Use Waiting Time

Read, memorize, check your planner as you wait in line. How many minutes/hours do you spend in line weekly? Use waiting time to get small tasks done.

Don't Let Perfectionism Stop You

Demanding perfection can be very self-defeating. Perfectionism can lead to paralysis which prevents the completion of activities. Guard against perfectionism; it is seldom necessary for the completion of a task.

Learn to Delegate

If you are able to delegate tasks to others, it may be very helpful to the achievement of goals. Give clear instructions and timelines to others who support your efforts.

Use Time Wisely

Time is a limited resource. Be careful how you invest it. Are you making the most of your time?

Value Your Time

Do you have to clean your apartment the day before mid-term examinations? Remind yourself of your priorities and goals. Which activities lead to the completion of your goals?

Time on Internet and Phone

Be careful of the amount of time you spend on the Internet and your cell phone. Is this a productive use of your time?

What Are the Benefits of Attending a Community College?

The most important benefit of getting a community college education is the acquisition of knowledge which has the potential to transform your life. Many community college students attend school for the purpose of re-directing their lives. Students are looking for purpose, meaning, goals, values, and what to do with the rest of their lives. The community college is an excellent environment for individuals wishing to direct or re-direct their lives. At the community college, you can assess who you are, what you are, and for what you are best suited.

Another major benefit of attending a community college is the cost. The cost of a community college education has not increased significantly in the last decade, although recent state budgetary problems are producing pressure to increase tuition at community colleges. The cost of obtaining a bachelor's degree is rising faster than the cost of obtaining an associates degree. Even though the tuition at community colleges varies widely from state to state, it is cost effective to pursue a community college education.

There are many other benefits to consider when choosing to attend the community college. Open access to community colleges provides equal opportunity to students pursuing advanced training and education. Community colleges provide a series of services to support student success. Access to a local community college provides a convenient and practical option for pursuing a college education. Reduced class size at community colleges greatly increases direct attention from professors and active participation in the learning process. The quality of a community college education is assured by local boards of trustees, accreditation and the accreditation process, outstanding faculty, and internal review procedures of programs and services.

21   What Is the Value of a Community College Degree?

The monetary value of a community college degree is significantly greater than the value of a high school diploma. A community college degree will increase your earning potential. Holders of associate's degrees are more apt to be interviewed for jobs and consequently hired because of a "screening effect." Employers want to interview degree holders. Credentials matter in the job market.

Holders of an associate's degree earn on average $250,000 more in their lifetime than those with a high school diploma. The federal government reports that the holder of a two-year degree will earn an average of $8,328 per year more than a high school graduate. The figure for the holder of a one year certificate of achievement is $3,780 annually.

The 1997 U.S. Census reports median earnings for persons 18 or older by educational attainment:

No high school diploma: $17, 148
High school graduate (includes equivalency): $22, 502
Some college, no degree: $26,090
Associate's degree: $29,457
Bachelor's degree: $36,525
Master's degree: $45,053
Professional degree: $65, 916
Doctorate: $56,758

The Bureau of Labor Statistics projects that between 2000-2010 among the fastest growing occupations and occupations with plentiful job openings are those requiring workers with an associate's degree.

The personal value of an associate's degree is immeasurable. Community college students re-direct and change their lives. Students actualize their potential. Parents become better parents by learning about child development. Managers become better managers by learning leadership skills. Employees become better employees by acquiring new job skills.

What Can I Expect the First Day of Class?

The first day of class is usually very exciting and interesting because it establishes the foundation and point of departure for many new learning and life experiences. You will be presented with challenges and opportunities to learn and grow. You may also meet others and form friendships that last a lifetime.

It is extremely important that you attend the first day of class because you may be dropped if you do not attend.

Be on time

Make sure you understand class requirements

Make sure you know what textbook and materials you will need for the class

Know what is expected of you

Review the syllabus, assignments, test dates, and due dates

Bring supplies

Know your instructor's name

Know where to park your car

Know where your classes are located

Meet students in your classes

Don't interrupt by coming late and leaving early

Know your instructor's name, office hours, location, phone number, and e-mail address

Developing
Your
Educational
Plan

## CHAPTER 2

STUDENT EDUCATIONAL PLAN

Name _____   Student Identification Number _____

Educational Goal _____   Major _____   Degree Goal _____

PLANNED COURSE SEQUENCE

Sem/Qtr.	Year	Units
Total Units		

Sem/Qtr.	Year	Units
Total Units		

Alternative Courses

PLANNED COURSE SEQUENCE

Sem/Qtr.	Year	Units
Total Units		

Sem/Qtr.	Year	Units
Total Units		

Alternative Courses

Major Courses	C	IP	N
Totals			

Assessment Results	
Math	
English	
Reading	
Sequence of courses for Associate's/Transfer Math	

Date _____

Academic Years _____   Community College _____

Transfer Institution _____   Certificate Program _____   Career Goal _____

PLANNED COURSE SEQUENCE

Sum Session/Qtr.	Year	Units
Total Units		

Sum Session/Qtr.	Year	Units
Total Units		

Alternative Courses

PLANNED COURSE SEQUENCE

Sum Session/Qtr.	Year	Units
Total Units		

Sum Session/Qtr.	Year	Units
Total Units		

Alternative Courses

Sequence of courses for Associate's/Transfer English

	Year 1	Year 2
Total degree applicable units completed		
Total units in progress		
Total units remaining		
Degree applicable cumulative GPA		
Transferable credits completed		
Non-Transferable credits completed		
Non-Degree applicable credits completed		
Core curriculum areas completed		
Core curriculum areas remaining		
Certification plan areas completed		
Certification plan areas remaining		

23 What Is the Academic Planning Process?

The academic planning process starts with you. Everything begins with you. Academic planning is a process designed to help you achieve your academic goals. The major product of this process is an educational plan designed to get you where you want to go. A major aspect of this process consists of meeting with an advisor. The advisor will play a major role in the development of your educational plan. Remember, it is your responsibility to finalize and implement this plan.

You will complete most of the activities of the academic planning process on your own. However, it is a very good idea to seek assistance whenever necessary. You will start with self-assessment including the assessment of your educational background. You will set goals, gather information, use the college catalog and Schedule of Classes, meet with an advisor, select a course of study, and review articulation agreements and curriculum guides. You may use the Internet to help develop an educational plan. The academic planning process will help you achieve your academic goals.

24 What Are the Elements of the Academic Planning Process?

Self-Assessment

Self-assessment involves the evaluation of previous educational background, work experience, and life experience. Self-assessment is frequently conducted with various forms of testing such as achievement, career, personality, and college academic placement. Self-assessment involves self-evaluation and deciding what you want out of life.

Assessment of Educational Background

Assessment of high school transcripts provides important information regarding academic planning at the college level.

Goal Setting

Goal setting is the process which brings academic planning into focus. The purpose of academic planning is the achievement of goals. Goals are written statements of what you want stated in desired outcomes.

Information Gathering

Information gathering provides the basis for academic planning. Connecting academic plans with career goals involves information gathering.

The Catalog

Reading your college catalog provides much of the information you need for academic planning. Your catalog contains course descriptions, degree requirements, certificate requirements, transfer requirements, and college policy information. Your catalog is your primary planning tool.

The Schedule of Classes

Reviewing the Schedule of Classes gives you the most immediate information on the current quarter/semester program. The Schedule of Classes contains the current academic program listed by subject alphabetically with a numerical system to identify each course. Each course offered is listed with instructor name, units, time, and location.

Meeting with Your Advisor

Prior to meeting with your academic advisor, do your homework. Be prepared and bring a list of questions to discuss with your advisor. Review relevant materials before your appointment, discuss your educational plan with your advisor, and ask your advisor for recommendations regarding the completeness and accuracy of your educational plan.

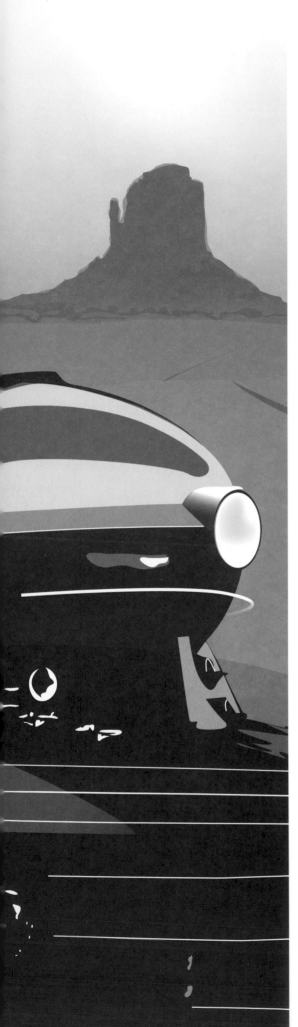

Course of Study

Decide on your course of study by completing all the elements of the academic planning process. Each element adds to your understanding of the academic process. Use your catalog and Schedule of Classes when you plan your semester/quarter program.

Articulation Agreements

Articulation agreements are documents used by your advisor to give you accurate information about the articulation of courses and transfer requirements. Articulation agreements are between your community college and carefully selected four-year colleges and universities. You may want to review articulation agreements included in your college catalog, on the web, and with your advisor. These agreements guarantee acceptance of your course work, general education, and courses in your major.

Curriculum Guides

Curriculum guides are frequently single page documents which contain academic requirements. They are available in your counseling center and transfer center. The guides provide an easy method to learn the set of academic requirements that apply to you. They may be on a single sheet of paper, a booklet, and/or brochures. Take them with you and learn your academic requirements.

Internet

The Internet can provide you with an enormous amount of information. Transfer information is readily available. Identify websites which are most relevant to you. Visit websites of the colleges that interest you.

Educational Plan

An educational plan at the community college usually consists of four or five semesters of full-time course work. These plans have great variation depending on the student. A part-time student will have a much longer educational plan. Student educational plans can consist of two years or more of courses leading to an educational goal. Each course on the educational plan is selected on the basis of meeting student educational goals such as associate degree requirements, certificate requirements, transfer requirements, and the attainment of other student educational goals.

25 What Are the Principal Academic Planning Tools?

College Catalog

There are several materials you will need to plan an academic program, but the two most important are the college Catalog and the college Schedule of Classes. The college Catalog contains a description of the classes you want to take, along with the number of units for each course, prerequisites, if any, and whether the course is transferable to four-year colleges and universities. The college Catalog also contains information regarding policies and procedures, including grading policies, degree requirements, types of programs offered, majors, an outline of student rights, and a student grievance procedure. Frequently, the Catalog contains information about the faculty. Grading policies may be of special interest to you, and you should make sure you know your rights as a student.

Schedule of Classes

The college Schedule of Classes is the college academic program for that particular semester/quarter. Courses that are going to be offered usually appear in alphabetical order along with the numbers of sections, course name, course number, number of units, location, and days and times courses will be offered. The college's Schedule of Classes contains a range of information useful to new, continuing, and returning students. For example, the registration procedure, degree requirements, transfer requirements, financial aid, student support programs and services, and some of the college academic policies are frequently included. Of special importance is the calendar for the semester. This calender contains important dates such as registration deadlines, holidays, and the final examination schedule. You need to know the first day of instruction, last day to drop a course without penalty, refund dates, and several other important dates. Don't forget to check the deadline for your graduation

application. Keep in mind that not all the courses you see in the college Catalog will appear in the college Schedule of Classes. Colleges do not offer every approved course listed in the Catalog every semester. It is beyond the scope of most colleges to offer every approved course every semester.

Your Catalog Year

Buy a Catalog. The catalog year when you enter college is especially important because it contains the requirements that will apply to you. Interruptions and absences from continuous enrollment can change your catalog year and therefore your requirements, and long absences from college enrollment can significantly affect your program requirements.

The Shortest Path

A major principle of academic planning is that of expediency. Many community college students have limited time and money to devote to their college education. Therefore, having a precise academic plan can be very beneficial. Usually, you want to take courses which result in progress towards your academic goals. Clear academic goals will help you in devising course loads for each semester of your program of study.

26 What Are the Major Educational Goals at the Community College?

Knowing your educational goals will help you determine your general education direction. Upon entering the community college, many students specify a desire to transfer to a university after completing a two-year community college degree. Identify the goals which seem appropriate to you at this time. Are you a community college transfer student? Or are you a vocational, job skills development, English acquisition, or a basic skills development student? What other reasons do you have for attending your community college?

Community College Student Educational Goals

_____ 1. Bachelor's degree after completing Associate of Arts (AA), Associate of Science (AS), Associate of Applied Science (AAS), and Associate of General Studies (AGS) Other _____

_____ 2. Bachelor's degree without completing AA/AS/AAS/AGS
Other _____

_____ 3. Two-year Associate's degree without transfer

_____ 4. Two-year vocational degree without transfer

_____ 5. Earn vocational certificate without transfer or a certificate of completion

_____ 6. Formulate career interests, plans, or goals

_____ 7. Prepare for new career (acquire job skills)

_____ 8. Advance in current job/career (update skills)

_____ 9. Maintain certificate/license (e.g., nursing, etc.)

_____ 10. Educational development

_____ 11. Improve basic skills in English, reading, math

_____ 12. Complete credits for high school diploma or GED

27 How Do I Develop an Educational Plan?

Developing an educational plan which maximizes your success, abilities, and potential requires a careful examination of your previous educational experience. Your high school performance and record (courses, and grades) is an important factor in developing an educational plan. Answer the following questions designed to give a brief profile of your high school background.

1. What was your high school grade point average (GPA)? _____

2. Were you a college prep student in high school? Yes/No

3. What was the last English course you had in high school? _____
    What was your grade? _____

4. What was the last math course you had in high school? _____
    What was your grade? _____

5. What was your favorite subject in high school? _____

6. Name the sciences you took in high school?

    _____   _____

    _____   _____

7. Did you take a foreign language in high school? Yes/No
    Which language? _____ How many years? _____

8. If you are pursuing a certificate program, name you major. _____

9. If you are pursuing an academic subject area, name your major. _____

10. Are you currently employed? Yes/No How many hours do you work per week? _____

11. List three jobs you have had in the last few years.

    _____
    _____

12. What are your career goals?

    _____
    _____
    _____

What Are Magic Numbers?

Magic numbers are important numerical designations for requirements. Magic numbers are indicators of the attainment of academic goals. For example, the number 60 is a magic number for many community college students because 60 units are frequently the number required to earn a community college degree. Magic numbers illustrate the number of credit hours and courses required for degrees, programs, transfer, general education, certificates, and majors. By keeping magic numbers in mind, you can quickly determine what will be required of you in order to reach your goal. Magic numbers give an immediate measure of progress towards an academic goal. Learn and memorize what will be required of you and keep track of your progress. This will give you a sense of movement toward your goals. Attainment of a magic number may transform your life. Therefore, they are magical. What are your magic numbers?

MAGIC NUMBERS

1. The number of units required for an Associate of Arts (AA), an Associate of Science (AS) degree and an Associate of Applied Science (AAS) is _____ (or other degree).

2. The minimum number of units required for a certificate program is _____.

3. The number of units required of a community college transfer student to university, state university, state college, or private college is _____, _____, _____, _____.

4. The minimum grade point average (GPA) to earn an associate degree is _____.

5. The minimum grade point average (GPA) required to transfer to a university, state university, state college, or private college is _____, _____, _____, _____.

6. The number of general education courses and units required for an Associate of Arts (AA) degree is _____ and _____.

7. The number of general education courses and units required for an Associate of Science (AS) degree is _____ and _____.

8. The number of general education courses and units required to transfer to a state university is _____ and _____.

9. The number of general education courses and units required to transfer to a state college is _____ and _____.

10. If you are pursuing a certificate program, how many courses must you take _____? And how many units must you complete _____?

11. How many math courses must you take to transfer to a university, state university, state college, or private college? _____, _____, _____, and _____.

12. Name competency requirements for an AA degree. _____
    Name competency requirements for an AS degree. _____
    Name competency requirements for an AAS degree. _____

13. How many units of a lab science do you need for a AA, AS, or AAS degree? _____

14. How many units of a lab science do you need to transfer to a university, state university, state college, or private college? _____, _____, _____, and _____.

29 How Do I Calculate My Grade Point Average?

Grade point average (GPA) is calculated on the basis of a grade point system. Each letter grade is assigned a grade point value. For example, an "A" is worth 4 grade points, a "B" is worth 3 grade points, a "C" is worth 2 grade points, a "D" is worth 1 grade point, and an "F" is worth 0 grade points. The grade point value of each letter grade is multiplied times the number of units. For example, an "A" in a 3 unit course is worth 12 grade points, a "B" in a 3 unit course is worth 9 grade points, a "C" is worth 6 grade points, a "D" is worth 3 grade points, and an "F" is worth 0 grade points. Total the grade points for each letter grade, including "Fs", and divide by attempted units. This gives you your GPA.

A = 4 grade points

B = 3 grade points

C = 2 grade points

D = 1 grade point

F = 0 grade points

GPA = total grade points / attempted units

Keep in mind, that credit/no credit repeated courses, incompletes, and audit courses are not assigned grade points, therefore, are not part of GPA calculation.

Example:

Subject	Units	Grade		Grade Points (Quality Points)
Psych 101	3	A	x	4 = 12
Soc 101	3	B	x	3 = 9
Engl 101	3	C	x	2 = 6
Math 115	3	D	x	1 = 3
Total Units = 12		Total Grade Points = 30		

Divide   30 ÷ 12 =2.5

GPA = 2.5

Grade Point Average

A = 4.0   B = 3.0   C = 2.0   D = 1.0   F = 0

73

How Do I Choose a Major?

You hesitated to enroll in your local community college because you hadn't decided on a major or field of study and you thought it would be a waste of time to get started without a major. To your surprise, you realized that you didn't have to wait to get started. Many students enter the community college without declaring a major. It takes time and exposure to the college environment, programs, subjects, and services to decide on a major. Many activities and guidelines can assist you in choosing a major. Foremost is deciding on what you want out of life, family, work, and school. Discovering your life's purpose and constructing a vision for your life will help direct you into areas of study. What is your passion? What drives you? What makes you get out of bed in the morning? How do you spend your time? How you respond to these questions is a starting point. Examine the following guidelines to help you choose a major:

- **Set Goals**

- **Focus on Interests**

- **Examine Values**

- **Identify Talents, Strengths, and Accomplishments**

- **Use General Education as a Vehicle to Identify a Major**

- **Take a Student Development Course**

- **Identify and Participate in College Mentoring Programs**

- **Use Campus Resources**

- **Pursue Further Evaluation**

Choosing a Major

- *Set Goals:* Goals are the key elements of a plan. When you set goals to determine your direction, they will help you determine a major.

- *Focus on Interests:* Focusing on your interests will help you get and stay motivated. Interests form a strong basis for life direction.

- *Examine Values:* Evaluate what gives meaning and purpose to your life. Values are a guide for the decision-making process. What will you study based on your values?

- *Identify Talents, Strengths, and Accomplishments:* You can choose a major based on your talents, strengths, and accomplishments. What are your talents, strengths, and accomplishments? Which majors are related to your talents, strengths, and accomplishments?

- *Use General Education as a Vehicle to Identify a Major:* General Education courses will expose you to a broad range of subjects, topics, and ideas. You may discover problems and issues which are most relevant to you and subsequently activate your interest and desire to make further inquiry.

- *Take a Student Development Course:* Many colleges offer a broad range of personal development courses which focus on issues that pertain to college students. They may include college success and career development goals.

- *Identify and Participate in College Mentoring Programs:* There are many benefits in having a mentor. The most significant benefit is being able to learn from the experience of your mentor. Mentors provide information, support, knowledge, and perspective.

- *Use Campus Resources:* The resources of your campus may be one of your greatest assets. They include the faculty of your college who may make a major contribution to your life. The resources include the library, counseling center, career center, financial aid office, and many other student support services.

- *Pursue Further Evaluation:* See a counselor and determine whether taking a battery of tests would be helpful in identifying your interests, values, personality type, occupational preferences, strengths, weaknesses, and goals.

75

31 What Majors Are Offered at the Community College?

Review this list of majors and programs. Check any of these which could be possible majors for you. Seek information including curriculum guides for selected majors and programs.

_____ Accounting

_____ Administration of Justices

_____ Administrative Aide

_____ Advertising

_____ African-American Studies

_____ Agriculture

_____ Air Conditioning/Refrigeration

_____ Alcohol/Drug Studies

_____ Anthropology

_____ Architectural Design

_____ Architectural Drafting

_____ Architecture

_____ Art

_____ Asian Studies

_____ Automotive

_____ Aviation Maintenance

_____ Behavioral Science

_____ Bilingual/Cross Cultural

_____ Biology

_____ Business

_____ Chemistry

_____ Chicano Studies

_____ Child Development

_____ Cinema

_____ Computer Programming

_____ Computer Sciences

_____ Communication

_____ Communicative Disorders

_____ Construction Technology

_____ Cosmetology

_____ Court Reporting

_____ Criminal Justice

_____ Culinary Arts

_____ Dance

_____ Dental Assistant

_____ Dental Hygiene

_____ Diesel Mechanics

_____ Drafting Technology

_____ Economics

_____ Electronics

_____ Emergency Medical Service

_____ Engineering

_____ English

_____ Environmental Hazardous/ Materials Technology

_____ Environmental Sciences

_____ Ethnic and Special Studies

_____ Exotic Animal Training and Management

_____ Fashion Design/ Merchandising

_____ Fire Technology

_____ Foreign Language

_____ General Studies

_____ Geography

_____ Geology

_____ Graphic Comm/Design Production

_____ Graphic Design Program

_____ Health Science

_____ High School Special Ed. Program

_____ History

_____ Home Economics

_____ Horticulture

_____ Hotel and Restaurant Management

_____ Human Services

_____ Illustration Program

_____ Industrial Maintenance Technology
_____ Industrial Safety
_____ Information Processing Systems
_____ Interior Design
_____ Journalism
_____ Laser/Electro-optics Technology
_____ Latin America Studies
_____ Legal Assisting
_____ Liberal Arts
_____ Logistics
_____ Machine Technology
_____ Mathematics
_____ Medical Data
_____ Medical Laboratory Technology
_____ Mexican-American Studies
_____ Microcomputer Specialist
_____ Mortuary Science
_____ Multi-Media
_____ Music
_____ Networking
_____ Nursing
_____ Occupational Therapy
_____ Office Technology/Secretarial
_____ Petroleum Technology
_____ Pharmacy Technology
_____ Philosophy
_____ Photography: Commercial
_____ Physical Education
_____ Physical Therapy Assistant

_____ Political Science
_____ Pre-Dental
_____ Pre-Law
_____ Pre-Medical
_____ Pre-Nursing
_____ Pre-Occupational Therapy
_____ Pre-Pharmacy
_____ Pre-Physical Therapy
_____ Psychiatric Technology
_____ Psychology
_____ Public Relations
_____ Radio-Television-Film
_____ Radiologic Technology
_____ Real Estate
_____ Religious Studies
_____ Respiratory Care
_____ Sociology
_____ Speech
_____ Surgical Technology
_____ Teaching/Liberal Studies
_____ Telecommunication
_____ Theater Arts
_____ Travel and Tourism
_____ Truck Operations
_____ Undecided-Undeclared
_____ Urban Studies
_____ Vocational
_____ Water Science
_____ Welding
_____ Women's Studies
_____ Other

What Degrees Are Offered by the Community College?

Community colleges offer multiple associate degrees which vary in their designations depending on the college, district, and state. The most common designations are Associate of Arts and Associate of Science degrees. Many colleges offer various two-year degrees. For example, Central Oregon Community College offers an Associate of General Studies (AGS) and Associate of Applied Science (AAS), in addition to the Associate of Arts (AA) and Associate of Science (AS) degrees.

Kishwaukee College offers Associate of Arts, Associate of Science, Associate of Applied Science, Associate in Engineering Science, Associate in Fine Arts (Fine Arts emphasis), and Associate in Fine Arts (Art Education emphasis) degrees. The Associate in Applied Science is a commonly offered degree in many community colleges in different states. Most frequently the AAS degree is an occupational, technical, professional, and/or job preparation degree.

 # What Is the Difference between Associate Degrees?

The major difference between degrees is their emphasis and purpose. Is the degree designed for transfer or is it designed for more immediate professional, occupational, and/or job objectives? Many associate degrees result in the fulfillment of requirements for admission to state colleges and universities. They are designed to be parallel. Many associate degrees are not 100 percent parallel with transfer requirements. Some colleges require the completion of prerequisites before entrance into a degree program. You may have to complete courses which are not degree applicable in order to enter a degree program. Many community colleges offer degrees which complete most of the requirements of their transfer institutions; therefore, it is important to meet with an advisor to make sure you are fulfilling all transfer requirements. Keep in mind that community colleges do not offer bachelor degrees.

Examine your educational goals to determine the type of degree which is most appropriate for you. Is your primary goal to transfer or is to acquire technical and occupational skills for career and job placement? Examine the pathways for additional help in selecting a degree appropriate for your needs.

Declaration of Major

Some community colleges require that you declare a major within a specified period of time. Others do not require a formal declaration of major. Most community colleges will ask you upon entrance to the college to declare a major. Many students are undecided. See choosing a major earlier in this chapter.

34 Why Do I Have to Take General Education?

Many students ask this question because they do not see the relevance of general education to their chosen field of study. They see it as a waste of time. Most degree programs at community colleges require completion of a body of courses called General Education Courses. This education pattern consists of the major academic disciplines with specific subject requirements. General Education usually includes requirements in English, Mathematics, Humanities, Sciences, Social and Behavioral Sciences, Physical Education and Health, and other learning skills subjects. Your community college may also have Ethnic Studies and/or Women Studies requirements. The Fine Arts are usually in the Humanities area, and Science requirements may consist of both Physical and Life Science. You may have to complete a laboratory course along with your science courses.

Why should you be required to complete General Education? The following reasons may help you see the importance and relevance of General Education:

1. *General Education Increases Your Knowledge and Skills.* By studying a variety of subjects, you will be exposed to new ideas and perspectives.
2. *General Education Helps You Learn to Think Critically.* Learning to think critically will help you address important life issues from a more thoughtful perspective.
3. *General Education Helps You Understand the World and Life.* The more informed you are about the world around you, the more able you are to understand people, events, ideas, and change.
4. *General Education Increases the Enjoyment and Appreciation of Life.* When you understand how something works, the more you will enjoy and appreciate it.

79

5. *General Education Allows You to Contribute More to Your Family.* You enrich the experience of your family by sharing your knowledge of various subjects.

6. *General Education Increases Knowledge, and Knowledge is Power.* The knowledge you acquire through General Education study will give you power and control over your life.

7. *General Education Will Help You Learn About Yourself.* Many courses in college initiate a process of self-discovery. Many different courses help you learn about yourself.

The following paragraph from the Joliet Junior College 2002 catalog describes the importance of General Education. This view is widely shared throughout the national community college system.

"The purpose of general education is to develop individuals who have sensitivity for an understanding of the world around them. A comprehensive general education will help students develop moral values, critical thinking skills, and investigate query that will prepare them well for a rapidly changing world. Generally, educated students possess the ability to communicate well, understand the scientific process and scientific inquiry, reason mathematically, appreciate the diverse cultures of the world, respect human history, and perceive the dynamics of human ethics and morality."

35   What Is a Certificate of Achievement?

A "Certificate of Achievement" is a recognition and certification of completion of a community college vocational/occupational program. It is believed that the completion of a certificate program signifies a level of mastery of skills associated with a vocational/occupational area. These programs usually give you the option of earning a vocational/occupational associate's degree. Your vocational/occupational program is the equivalent of your major. For example, you can earn a certificate in auto technology, fire technology, air conditioning, diesel mechanics, and many others. Many certificate programs are comprised of eight required courses, but there is great variation in the number of courses and units required for certificate programs. If you are interested in a vocational/occupational program, see your advisor.

36   What Is a Certificate of Completion?

A "Certificate of Completion" is a recognition of completion of an organized program of vocational study. These programs usually require a minimum number of units completed in the major. Unlike a Certificate of Achievement, Certificates of Completion are more limited in scope, usually require less units, and often awarded in job training.

How Do I Choose a Vocational/ Occupational Program?

In selecting a vocational/occupational program, it is very important to follow your interests, values, and aptitudes. It is important to assume the question, why? Why have you selected a particular vocational/occupational program? Some experience and background associated with your program of choice is an important preliminary step. Making a selection of a vocational program is a major commitment. You are committing time, resources, and energy when you pursue a program of study. Frequently, it is possible to take the introductory course to a vocational/occupational program. You may want to find out what a program is all about before you make a full commitment.

Where will this program lead you? Is there a job waiting at the completion of the program? Does your college help you with job placement? What is the employment rate of graduates of this program? Think your decision through before you select and commit to a vocational/occupational program. See your vocational counselor and consider your options carefully.

38

How Do I Transfer to a Four–Year College or University?

The transfer process is a transitional period for community college students wishing to pursue a bachelor's degree at a four-year college or university. Transferring to a four-year institution may seem extremely complicated and overwhelming. Therefore, it is useful to reduce the transfer process into simplified terms and key elements.

Articulation

Many community college courses are articulated to four-year colleges and universities. This simply means that four-year colleges and universities agree to recognize and accept those identified courses from the community college. These courses are college level, baccalaureate level courses, which are deemed equivalent to courses offered by the four-year college and university. These courses appear on "articulation agreements" between the colleges. Major requirements and general education courses are generally articulated to four-year colleges or universities.

Core Curriculum

Many colleges and universities require community college transfer students to complete an articulated core curriculum pattern as part of the admissions process. Core curriculum is a body of general education courses which a transfer student needs to complete prior to transfer.

Transfer Credit

A transfer student accumulates transfer credit by taking courses which are articulated to the four-year institution of choice.

Key Elements for Transfer

A transfer student is frequently accepted to a four-year institution on the basis of transfer credit earned, completion of a core curriculum, general education, certification plans, and completion of major course requirements. It is possible to be admitted to a four-year college without being admitted to a department (major of choice). Meet with a representative of the institution to which you plan to transfer.

Transfer Degrees

Many community colleges offer Associate of Arts and Associate of Science degrees which meet the admissions requirements of local colleges and universities. The community college and the four-year institution have articulation agreements which acknowledge and accept transfer associate degrees. Furthermore, some states have statewide articulation initiatives which guarantee acceptance of transfer courses, credit hours, degrees, and admission. Some programs leading to an associate degree are college parallel and allow the recipient to transfer with advanced standing to a four-year institution.

What Is the Transfer Procedure?

- Obtain a catalog of your selected transfer institution. Review the admissions requirements for community college transfers, including general education requirements and courses required in your major.

- Meet with your college counselor each semester/quarter and conjointly develop an educational plan.

- University representatives frequently visit community colleges and provide sessions for students. Schedule an interview with representatives from prospective transfer institutions.

- Ascertain appropriate filing dates to apply to your selected transfer institution. Many colleges/universities allow on-line Internet application procedures. Forward your community college transcripts at the appropriate time.

- Visit your transfer institution. This will give you direct experience of the college/university for which you will make a major life decision. Visit the department of your selected major. If possible, meet the dean of your department. Talk with students who are already attending your prospective college. Arrange to meet with an advisor prior to your visit.

- Take your transcripts and catalog to facilitate your advisory meeting.

- If you change your major, make an appointment with your counselor to determine how this will change your transfer preparation.

- Most community college transfer students will not follow the catalog of their selected transfer institution but follow a prescribed core curriculum pattern, certification plan, or an articulated associate transfer degree. This is especially true for new students attending community college for the first time. Students who have attended many community colleges are more likely to follow the catalogue of their selected transfer institution.

A General Transfer Flow Chart

STUDENT ENTERS COMMUNITY COLLEGE
(Plans to transfer to a Four-Year Institution)

CLASS STANDING
0 UNITS

FRESHMEN
30 UNITS
45 QTR. UNITS

SOPHOMORE
60 UNITS
90 QTR. UNITS

LOWER DIVISION PROGRAM
GENERAL EDUCATION
PREREQUISITES FOR MAJOR
ELECTIVES
CERTIFICATION PLANS
CORE CURRICULUM

ASSOCIATE DEGREE NON-TRANSFER

ASSOCIATE DEGREE TRANSFER

CLASS STANDING
60 UNITS
90 QTR. UNITS

JUNIOR
90 UNITS
120 QTR. UNITS

SENIOR
120 UNITS
180 QTR. UNITS

UPPER DIVISION PROGRAM
UPPER DIVISION G.E.
CONCENTRATION ON MAJOR
ELECTIVE UNITS
SELECTION OF OPTIONS

APPROX. 124+ UNITS (180 Qtr. Units)

**B.A. BACHELOR'S OF ARTS
B.S. BACHELOR'S OF SCIENCE**

**M.A. MASTER'S OF ARTS
M.S. MASTER'S OF SCIENCE**

DOCTOR OF PHILOSOPHY (Ph.D.)

40 What Is the General Education Certification Plan?

In California, community college students have the option of completing transfer requirements for the California State University and the University of California systems by completing the transfer General Education Certification Plan (CSU) and the Intersegmental General Education Transfer Curriculum (IGETC) (UC). The IGETC may also be used by CSU students. Students going to CSU must complete 56 or 60 transferable units and 60 transferable units for UC.

General Education Certification Plan (CSU)

The CSU Certification Plan requires the completion of approximately thirteen courses consisting of:

Area A   (3 courses)
         Communication and Critical Thinking

Area B   (3 courses)
         Physical Universe and Its Life Forms

Area C   (3 courses)
         Arts, Foreign Language, Humanities, Literature

Area D   (3 courses)
         Social, Political, Economic, Institutions & Behavior,
         Historical Background

Area E   (1 or 2 courses)
         Lifelong Understanding and Self-Development

American Institution Requirement (A.I.R.)

The CSU System requires one course in American History and one course in American Government. These courses can be used to partially fulfill requirements for Area D. Students must complete a science including a laboratory course, and a college level mathematics course. Foreign language courses may be used to partially fulfill Area C requirements even though students are not required specifically to take a foreign language. There are other options for fulfilling Area C requirements.

 # What Is the Intersegmental General Education Transfer Curriculum?

The IGETC requires the completion of approximately twelve courses consisting of the following areas:

Area 1   (2 courses)
           English Communication

Area 2   (1 course)
           Mathematical Concepts & Quantitative Reasoning

Area 3   (3 courses)
           Arts & Humanities

Area 4   (3 courses)
           Social & Behavioral Sciences

Area 5   (2 courses and 1 laboratory)
           Physical & Biological Sciences

Area 6   (2nd semester college level course)
           Languages other than English

The IGETC requires completion of two sciences and a laboratory, designated university level mathematics course, and a foreign language. Several options are allowed to fulfill the foreign language requirement.

The courses used on both the CSU Certification Plan and the IGETC are specific to your college. Check with your counselor and obtain copies of your Certification Plan and the IGETC.

42

What Is Assist?

Assist is a California State Community College computerized student transfer information system which is widely used by community college advisors/counselors and students to determine course requirements for their specific majors. This system does not include private universities and colleges. If you are a California resident, you can very quickly determine your major requirements and other information for a specific state college or university by clicking on www.assist.org.

43

What is the Illinois Articulation Initiative (IAI)?

If you are a community college transfer student in Illinois, it would be advantageous to determine whether your college is a participant in the Illinois Articulation Initiative (IAI). The (IAI) is designed to facilitate the transfer of credit and to allow the transfer of a set of courses called the General Education Core Curriculum to more than 100 participating public and private colleges and universities. The completion of this core curriculum results in a guarantee that transferring students will be granted the equivalent credit of the entire general education program of the receiving four-year college or university. For additional information on the core curriculum and the transferability of courses, consult the website www.Itransfer.org and consult with your college counselor. For students in other states, check with your counselor for articulation initiatives that apply to you.

44   How Are Transfer Courses Numbered?

Identifying the course numbering system of your community college may be a helpful guide in determining transferable courses. Meet with a counselor to determine the type of numbering system used at your community college. Check with your counselor to determine the usefulness of this guide. The college catalog will identify transfer level courses. Courses which are numbered 300 and 400 level are usually upper division, junior and senior level at the four-year institution.

45   How Do I Select a Transfer College or University?

Many students select a transfer institution on the basis of location. If it is nearby, they select that institution. Usually you want to go to the very best institution you can afford. That might not be the nearest college. Select an institution on the basis of your major. Is the college or university widely recognized in your major of choice? Visit the college or university you are considering. Never select a college/university you have not visited. Most important in selecting a four-year institution is talking with others about your choice. Talk with your professors, fellow students, and advisors regarding your prospective choices.

Connecting
with
Student
Services

## CHAPTER 3

46 What Are Student Services?

Community colleges are usually structured into two major components: instruction and student support services. Instruction is the major component and function of the community college, but without student support services, many students would fall by the wayside. Student support services exist to provide positive, meaningful, and helpful services to students. This function is designed to promote student success and retention. If you need help, think of student support services. Your college might provide a similar range of services, and it might use a different name for this function such as student development. Student support services provide a comprehensive set of services which include many of the following services listed:

Admissions and Records
•
Counseling Services
•
Re-Entry
•
Financial Aid
•
Bookstore
•
Writing Center
•
Career Center
•
Job Placement
•
Transfer Center
•
Specialized Support Services
•
Disabled Student Services
•
Health Services
•
Campus Security
•
Food Services

Admissions and Records

The admissions and records office of your college provides a range of services which directly impact you, the student. Admissions is concerned with the processing of applications which are used to determine admission into the college. Records is concerned with the maintenance of student transcripts, posting of grades, grade point average calculations and many other functions. The application process identifies you, the student, through a numbering system which is usually the social security numbering system. Community colleges are moving away from a wide use of social security numbers to identify students because of identity theft. Admissions performs the major function of registration. During the registration process, you identify, select, and enter (register) into courses. The Admissions and Records office is sometimes separated into two distinct offices, each concentrating on its primary functions:

- Application for admission
- Residency determination
- Transcripts
- Tuition assistance transcripts
- Veterans
- Certificates of Achievement
- Athletic eligibility
- Graduation checks
- Posting of military credit
- Incomplete grade changes
- GPA verifications
- Credit/No Credit applications
- Academic renewal

Counseling Services

Counseling departments in community colleges usually provide three major types of counseling services: academic advisement, career counseling, and personal counseling. Counselors are essential in helping you design your educational plan. They are trained professionals who can help you with goal setting, decision-making, academic information, major selection, time management, test anxiety, self-esteem, and many other student issues. Counseling services may include:

- Academic advisement
- Educational plans
- Career counseling
- Goal setting
- Academic information
- Decision making
- Career development
- Life skills
- Study skills
- Conflict resolution

Re-Entry

Re-entry programs are designed for both men and women. These programs are designed to assist students who are re-entering college after a lapse of time. Re-entry programs help students make a smooth transition back into academic life. Frequently, re-entry students are women defining who they are and seeking a new life direction. Re-entry programs provide:

- A supportive environment
- Counseling
- Referral services
- Workshops
- Lectures
- Programs
- Mentoring

Financial Aid

The financial aid office of the community college is designed to assist students through the financial aid application process. The financial aid office assembles financial aid packages for students based on availability, eligibility, and need. Checks are disbursed through the financial aid office. This office usually maintains files on students including the financial aid package, educational plan, and progress records. Both state and federal sources of financial aid are processed through the financial aid office. The financial aid office can help with:

- Grants
- Loans
- Work-study
- Federal aid
- State aid
- Application
- Fee waivers
- Eligibility
- VA benefits
- Disbursement of funds
- Datelines
- Scholarships
- Other sources of aid

Bookstore

Most community colleges have an on-campus college bookstore. The primary function of the bookstore is to provide students with required textbooks and materials for the college's courses. College bookstores provide many other products and services. Your college bookstore may provide many of the following products and services:

- Textbooks
- Supplies: pens, pencils, binders, paper, calendars, life planners, etc.
- Art supplies
- Supplies for vocational programs: Example: a cutlery set for the Hotel and Restaurant Management Program
- Computer hardware
- Computer software: academic pricing
- Electronic video games
- Clothing: sometimes with college monograms
- Backpacks
- Greeting cards
- Gift items / Wrapping
- UPS / FAX services
- Copy center
- Notary Public

Writing Center

Many community colleges have writing centers. The writing center can assist you in writing essays, reports, term papers, research papers, and other writing assignments. The writing center helps students understand the writing process. Students learn about writing styles, grammar and punctuation, organization techniques, and the overall correctness of writing projects. Services include:

- Instruction on writing
- Feedback on writing projects
- A place to write
- Resource

Career Center

Most community colleges have career centers which are designed to provide students with career information, career testing, and job placement. Career counselors perform comprehensive career evaluations which are designed to identify career options based on interests, values, and abilities. If you are confused about what to do with your life, visit your campus career center for:

- Career reference books
- Career information
- Career testing
- Computerized testing
- Computerized career searches
- Career counseling
- Career evaluation and analysis
- Job placement

Job Placement

Job placement services on your campus may be limited or comprehensive. It depends on your college. Some job placement offices are combined with the career center. Frequently, jobs on and off campus are available, and listings may be posted. You can make an appointment with a job placement counselor to help you find employment. You can learn about:

- Part-time employment on and off campus
- Employment in business and industry
- Employment in government agencies
- Employment in education

Transfer Center

Transfer centers provide materials and services to assist students through the transfer process. They maintain articulation agreements, core curriculum guides, major guides, internet access, and the latest information pertaining to transfer. The transfer counseling services are designed to help you develop an educational plan for transfer and provide:

- Transfer counseling
- Transfer workshops
- Application assistance
- Deadlines
- Transfer day visitations
- Counselor transfer institution appointments
- Transfer curriculum guides
- Major guides
- Internet access
- Certification guides
- Core curriculum guides
- Articulation agreements

Specialized Support Services

There are specialized student support services programs designed to help students succeed in college. These programs are either funded by the state or federal government. An example of a state sponsored program is the California Extended Opportunity Program and Services (EOPS.) Examples of federal programs are the TRIO programs such as Talent Search and Upward Bound. These programs serve specific student populations. Check with your counselor to determine for which support programs you qualify.

Disabled Student Services

The goal of Disabled Student Services is to help students with disabilities achieve their educational, occupational, career, and personal goals. Students with all types of disabilities are assisted.

Types of Disabilities:

- Vision
- Learning disabilities
- Mobility
- Speech
- Deaf/hard of hearing
- Head injuries
- Psychological disabilities
- Attention deficit disorder
- Back injuries, broken limbs
- Carpal tunnel syndrome
- Chronic illness

Services and Accommodations:

- Priority registration
- Academic "registration"
- Learning disability assessment
- Assistive technology
- Books on tape
- Braille transcription
- Disability related counseling
- Educational program advisement
- Enlarged print
- Equipment loans
- Job development/placement
- Learning skills classes
- Motorized carts
- Note-taking services
- Sign language interpreters
- Test-taking accommodations
- Tutoring
- Vocational counseling

Health Services

Most community colleges offer health services to students. Some states require student health fees paid at registration. Student health insurance may also be available at your college. Community colleges usually do not offer comprehensive health services but do offer:

- First aid / TB testing
- Diagnosis and treatment of illness
- Immunization
- Nutritional information
- Family planning
- Psychological services and substance abuse counseling
- Referral to community resources
- Appointment with a doctor, women's health specialist, nurse practitioner, dermatologist
- Health education workshops and lectures

Campus Security

Community colleges usually have safe and secure educational environments. Campus security is typically provided by the campus police. Many campuses maintain open visibility through good lighting and landscape maintenance. Most campus emergencies should be directed to the campus police. If you doubt, dial 911. Campus security usually will:

- Maintain lost and found property
- Patrol the campus
- Maintain criminal statistics
- Provide vehicular assistance

Food Services

Food services on community college campuses vary widely. Some community colleges have large cafeterias, while others have small food service concessions. Many offer hot and cold meals, and some offer gourmet services through the Hotel and Restaurant Management program. Check with your college to acquire information about food services on your campus. You'll probably find:

- Hot and cold meals
- Salad bar and grill
- Coffee specialties
- Breakfast, lunch and dinner
- Gourmet meals
- Patio eating areas
- Open day and evening

What Are the Major Community College Academic Policies?

It is especially important for you to understand the academic policies of your community college. Although these policies vary from college to college, there is remarkable similarity between colleges. Academic policies include matters of student attendance, grading practices, grading system, final examinations, auditing classes, withdrawal from college, course repetition, academic renewal, credit by examination, probation, dismissal, and re-admission, cheating or plagiarism, dean's list, and use of listening or recording devices. For further clarification of your college's academic policies, non-academic policies, and student rights, refer to your college catalog.

Attendance/Dropping Classes

Class attendance is important and required at community colleges. Attendance during the first week of class is essential and absences may result in administrative action resulting in the student being dropped from class. Absences usually count from the first class meeting after registration. Instructors are the primary persons who establish the attendance policy for their courses. During the first week of class, instructors delineate the attendance policy for their courses. For many instructors, tardiness or leaving early may be considered absences. Ultimately, instructors maintain attendance records and enforce their policies. In most instances, if you need to drop a class, it is your responsibility to complete the required drop form. It is not the instructor's responsibility to insure that you are dropped from class. Failure to officially drop a course or withdraw from the college may result in the student receiving an "F" in the course. Most instructors allow a minimum number or small percentage of absences. Many instructors allow a minimum of unexcused absences. Some community colleges expect students to notify their instructors when they are going to be absent. Accumulated absences may result in the student being dropped from the class.

Grading

Most community colleges use the traditional letter grade system to designate levels of academic performance. Keep in mind that there may be deviation from this system depending on the college. This is the traditional grading system.

Letter Grade	Grade Points
A Excellent	4
B Good	3
C Satisfactory	2
D Passing	1
F Not Passing/Failure	0
GPA	Grade Point Average
P/NP	Pass/Not Pass – not included in GPA calculation
CR/NC	Credit/No Credit – not included in GPA calculation
W	Withdrawal – not included in GPA calculation
WM	Military Withdrawal
IP	Course in progress
I	Incomplete – not included in GPA calculation
RD	Report delayed
A	Audit – not included in GPA calculation and does not meet academic requirements

P/NP and CR/NC are essentially the same grading option. Not all courses are offered under this option. Contact a college counselor to determine which courses are offered on a P/NP and CR/NC option.

Withdrawals are especially important because they are governed by deadlines with restrictions. If deadlines are not met a grade of "F" is frequently assigned. Make sure you know withdrawal dates.

Withdrawal from College

To withdraw from the college, a student must complete the official withdrawal form. These are usually available at the admissions and counseling offices.

Auditing Classes

A student who wants to enroll in a college credit course for personal enrichment and who does not want to earn college credit may elect to "audit" the course. See your college catalog for other requirements and stipulations regarding auditing.

Examinations

Final examinations are required and are held at the end of each term in accordance with the schedule issued by the registrar. When final examinations are inappropriate because of the nature of the course, exceptions to this requirement may be made. The final examination schedule is frequently presented in the college schedule of classes. Ask your instructors about final examinations regarding your course.

Credit by Examination

Under this policy students are allowed to earn college credit through examination. This frequently involves completing a petition and taking the final examination for a specific course. There are restrictions for the use of credit by examination. Usually, you cannot use credit by examination for courses in which you have taken more advanced courses. The intent of credit by examination is to allow the student to use equivalent experience to a specified course to earn college credit.

Course Repetition

Most courses may be repeated depending on your "grade" and when your course was taken. A course for which you earned a substandard grade may be repeated. This includes grades of "D" or "F". There are limitations to course repetitions. Check with your counselor.

Incomplete

A grade of incomplete ("I") indicates that satisfactory work has been done in a course, but the student has been prevented from completing the final examination or other concluding work because of some verifiable reason. The grade of "I" may be given as a final grade only. An "I" grade will not be given unless the student contacts his or her instructor and a contract for completion of work is approved. The "I" grade must be removed by the time specified in the college catalog.

Academic Renewal

Academic renewal is a mechanism for the elimination of substandard grades received in the past. Substandard grades include D's and F's. There are specific requirements to be eligible for academic renewal. Academic renewal is designed to eliminate substandard academic grades which are preventing a student from achieving present academic goals due to a low grade point average. See your counselor for clarification of this policy.

Use of Listening or Recording Devices

The use of tape recorders and other devices in community college classes may be restricted. Unlike four year colleges and universities which may allow liberal use of these devices, community colleges have policies which are delineated in the college catalog. One major exception is the right of students with disabilities to use devices in the classroom to enhance their learning. For further questions, ask your college instructors.

Dean's List

The Dean's List is reserved for students who have demonstrated exceptional academic performance. A grade point average of 3.5 or more is usually given special notice by colleges. The Dean's List is sometimes given other designations. Check with your counselor regarding special recognition for exceptional performance.

Progress Probation

Progress probation is an academic standing resulting from the non-completion of college work. Progress probation results from accumulating excessive withdrawals (W), incompletes (I), and no-credits (NC). The accumulation of more than 50 percent of incompletes, withdrawals, and no-credits when enrolled in a minimum of 12 units will result in progress probation. Progress probation status for two or more consecutive semesters may result in disqualification or dismissal. Like academic probation, a student who is disqualified may re-apply after one semester of non-attendance. Progress probation may have different designation at your college. Check with you advisor for further clarification.

Probation, Dismissal, and Re–Admission

Academic probation is based on a below minimum standard of academic performance as indicated by Grade Point Average. Commonly, anything below a 2.0 in at least 12 semester units attempted as illustrated on the college transcript results in academic probation. Academic probation is usually determined by cumulative Grade Point Average. Academic probation for a period of two or more semesters may result in disqualification or dismissal. Disqualified or dismissed students may be prohibited from enrolling in classes for one or more semesters. After one or more semesters without attending, a student may apply for re-admission. Academic probation policies vary from college to college. Check with your advisor for further clarification.

Cheating and Plagiarism

Community colleges have academic policies regarding cheating and plagiarism. Cheating on examinations is a significant offense, and the consequences of such action are stated in your college catalog under academic policies. Copying the work of others and presenting it as one's own is plagiarism and has significant penalties. There are several forms of cheating, and various methods of plagiaristic activity, and both are examples of academic dishonesty. Written, oral, and artistic work may be violated through plagiarism. Cheating on exams, placement tests, and using commercial research services are forms of academic dishonesty.

Behaving in an ethical manner is your responsibility, and an important part of education, and the issues of cheating and plagiarism should not enter your academic life.

Student Misconduct

It is your responsibility to behave in an appropriate and responsible manner as a community college student. A few students behave in not only inappropriate but also in unlawful ways. For example, the use of drugs is not tolerated on college campuses. Also, any form of rape will be referred to the appropriate authorities. Keep in mind that many colleges have a zero tolerance policy concerning drug use, and none condone date rape or other forms of abuse. In spite of occasional violations of college policies, colleges are usually safe, nurturing, and caring environments.

Conceptualizing Success

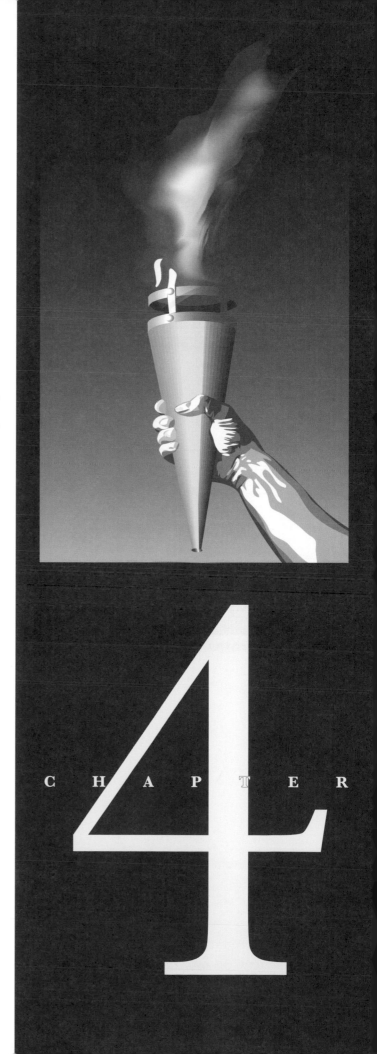

## CHAPTER 4

The Triadic System

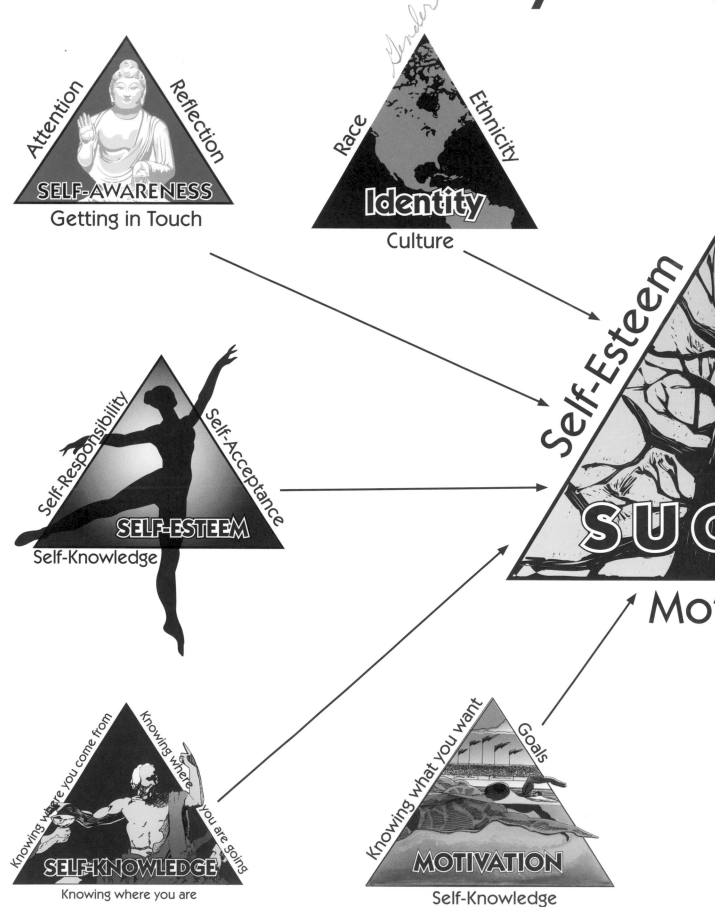

# of Success

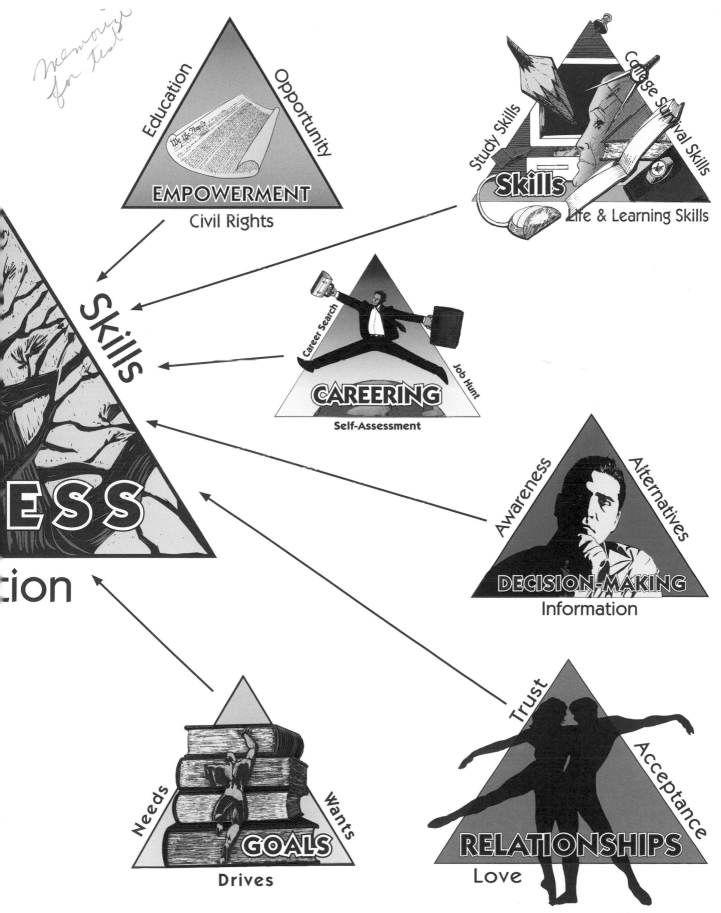

How Do I Achieve Success?

What is success to you? Are you on the road to success? How do you know that you're on the right road? The achievement of success has many roads.

Success is many things to many people. Some define success as the satisfactory completion of a goal. Others define it as gaining wealth and fame. Success is an individual determination and decision, although others can help clarify and direct our success. Sophocles said, "There is no success without hardship." And according to Robert Browning, "A minute's success pays the failure of years."

What are your thoughts about success? What is your approach to achieve success? Some individuals emphasize the habits and characteristics of successful people, while others focus on core beliefs. This book emphasizes the application of cognitive tools to transform your life. Take a cognitive tool, and apply it. Does it work for you? The cognitive system used in this book is called the Triadic System of Success.

People who succeed apply powerful cognitive tools. You can succeed by increasing motivation, developing positive self-esteem, and by acquiring a broad range of skills.

 ## 49 What Is The Triadic System of Success?

 ## 50 What Is The Success Triad?

The Triadic System is an integrated and comprehensive system of success. It consists of twelve triads and thirty-six factors associated with success. The Success Triad is the foundation of the Triadic System. The auxiliary triads support the three factors of the Success Triad: Motivation, Self-Esteem, and Skills. The Triadic System is interactive and interdependent and is comprised of success-achieving behaviors and concepts. The system identifies the factors which most contribute to success. The Triadic System is a conceptual system and tool used for cognitive self-appraisal. It provides tools for maximizing processes which form the foundation of success.

The Success Triad is a conceptual model for student success. It illustrates the success factors of Motivation, Self-Esteem, and Skills and forms a comprehensive basis for student success. The Success Triad is a framework for thinking about issues and problems regarding student performance. It developed from a synthesis of thought abstracted from counseling and classroom experience. It became evident that motivation and self-esteem in combination with the development of appropriate skills were vital to student success. The Success Triad is a product of intense attention and careful listening to students presenting issues relating to academic performance and personal conflict.

The Triads and Factors

The Empowerment Triad: Civil Rights, Education, and Opportunity, connects empowerment to these important factors. We learn that there is a social dimension to success and a free and just society is the basis of individual and collective success.

The Success Triad: Motivation, Self-Esteem, and Skills, forms a powerful basis for college and life success. Motivation is the driving force behind our efforts to succeed. Self-Esteem is associated with self-confidence and self-worth. Skills, based on knowledge, provide us with the tools to complete tasks effectively and efficiently.

The Motivation Triad: Self-Knowledge, Knowing what you want, and Goals, illustrates the importance of these factors in becoming motivated. Goals are the energizers of motivation. Self-Knowledge forms a powerful source of motivation, and knowing what you want is the basis for goal setting.

The Self-Esteem Triad: Self-Knowledge, Self-Responsibility, and Self-Acceptance, is the principal guide for developing and maintaining positive levels of self-esteem. Self-Knowledge is the foundation of positive levels of self-esteem. By taking self-responsibility and accepting ourselves, we establish our sense of self-worth.

The Skills Triad: Life and Learning Skills, Study Skills, and College Survival Skills, illustrates a broad spectrum of skills which promote life and college success. Skills enhance our level of performance and refine our problem-solving skills.

The Self-Knowledge Triad: Knowing where you are, Knowing where you come from, and Knowing where you are going, reveals the basis of self-knowledge. This Triad emphasizes that self-knowledge is the basis of life success.

The Self-Awareness Triad: Getting in Touch, Attention, and Reflection, demonstrates the value of getting in touch with experience, attending to experience, and reflecting on experience. We learn that self-awareness is the basis of self-knowledge.

The Goals Triad: Drives, Needs, and Wants, helps us determine our direction. Knowing our sources of motivation and knowing what we want and need allows us to set our goals. The Goals Triad helps us understand our motivation and set our course.

The Decision-Making Triad: Information, Awareness, and Alternatives, provides a basic decision-making model for us. The Decision-Making Triad illustrates the importance of taking control of one's life through decision-making.

The Identity Triad: Culture, Race, and Ethnicity, enables us to question our identity. We learn that identity has a strong social component. We see that identity is an important success issue, and who we are is the basis of our success.

The Relationship Triad: Love, Trust and Acceptance, presents a concise model for assessing relationships. We can examine our relationships on the basis of love, trust, and acceptance. The Relationship Triad is a basic model for evaluating our relationships.

The Careering Triad: Self-Assessment, Career Search, and Job Hunt, delineates the major stages of the careering process. This Triad illustrates that career development usually starts with self-assessment continues with a career search and culminates in a job hunt.

51 How Do You Apply The Triadic System of Success?

The Triadic System is a way to conceptualize success. It is applied by:

Examining

Clarifying

Questioning

Expanding

Extrapolating

Discussing

Implementing

the triads and factors of The Triadic System.

52 What Are the Success Factors of The Triadic System?

The Triadic System of Success assumes that the three success factors which most contribute to success are:

Motivation

Self–Esteem

Skills

Motivation, positive self-esteem, and skills lead to success.

How Are the Triads Used?

53

The Triadic System is used to identify and clarify how we can promote our success. For example, The Self-Esteem Triad emphasizes self-knowledge, self responsibility, and self-acceptance as the essentials of positive self-esteem. We can address these factors in our daily experience by questioning the triads and responding to the factors. "How do I assess and develop self-knowledge, self-responsibility and self-acceptance?" We apply The Triadic System by questioning the triads and applying them to ourselves.

Triads are:

Instruments for change

Cognitive and behavioral tools

Guides for evaluation and action

Problem–solving models

Theoretical systems

Road maps

Triads identify and clarify where you need to focus your energy in order to succeed.

 # How Do I Enhance Self–Esteem?

Real self-esteem is built on a foundation of truthfulness about who and what we are. A central issue in achieving and maintaining positive levels of self-esteem focuses on the principle of being in control of one's life. Being in charge of our lives through active decision-making and responsibility is essential for high levels of self-esteem.

To a large extent, how we think determines how we feel, and how we think and feel determine how we act. A careful examination of our self-concept can do much to increase our level of self-esteem. How we think about ourselves determines whether we see ourselves as worthy or unworthy. Learning to accept ourselves is the principal process by which we maintain adequate levels of self-esteem. The process for increasing self-esteem includes increasing self-awareness, self-knowledge, self-understanding, and self-acceptance.

Self-esteem is realistic self-respect derived from favorable self-impressions and positive impressions from others which contribute to our sense of self-worth.

Self–Esteem is enhanced by:

Accepting ourselves

Setting realistic expectations

Forgiving ourselves

Taking risks

Trusting ourselves and others

Expressing our feelings

Appreciating our creativity

Appreciating our spiritual being

Appreciating our minds

Appreciating our bodies

Taking responsibility for our decisions and actions

Being a person of integrity

Understanding and affirming our values

Attending to our physical health

Developing basic skills

Serving humanity

55 How Do I Get Motivated?

Everyone is motivated by something. Everyone wants to do something. What motivates you? What do you want to achieve? What do you want out of life? What drives you to act? What are you seeking? Motivation is the driving force behind our actions. Those forces are used to explain why we act the way we do. You get motivated by clearly identifying what you want. Knowing what you want gives your life direction. Doing what you want is much easier than doing what you have to. Staying focused on what you want tends to keep you motivated. Knowing what you want is the basis of goal setting, and goals are the energizers of motivation. The following types of motivation will help you understand how your behavior is activated.

General Motivation

Your general level of motivation is determined by your attitude and willingness to be actively involved in a broad range of activities. General levels of motivation reflect your state of being. Your general level of motivation is associated with your willingness to learn, grow, and change.

Intrinsic Motivation

Intrinsic motivation is the performance of activities for the rewards contained within the structure of the activity. The intrinsic motivation of acquiring an education is not the culmination of an earned degree, but the process of getting to the end result. The learning experiences which incorporate value, pleasure, meaning, competency, insights, and understanding constitute the intrinsic sources of motivation.

Extrinsic Motivation

Extrinsic motivation is the drive to perform activities for a desired result. The activity may not be meaningful or pleasurable, but one is constantly aiming for the result. Studying only to achieve high marks is a type of extrinsic motivation. The tennis player who plays only to win is motivated by extrinsic factors. The strength of the results determines our persistence in activities which are motivated by extrinsic factors. Power, prestige, and money can all be sources of extrinsic motivation.

Situation–Specific Motivation

In situation-specific motivation, the characteristics of the situation significantly impact on your willingness to respond. The situation elicits your behavior. You may be willing to do things in given situations that you would not customarily do. Your situational level of motivation might indicate a willingness to read English literature in a classroom, for example, but not alone at your desk at home.

Task–Specific Motivation

The characteristics of a particular task and your perception of that task determine your motivational level as you approach the task. What you find appealing, others may not find appealing. Thus, your perception of a task determines your level of motivation in regard to that task.

Motivation is enhanced by:

Awareness of drives

Knowing what you want

Staying focused on what you want

Awareness of the intrinsic value of activities

Awareness of the extrinsic value of activities

Awareness of triggers of action

Appeal of the task

Rewards

Surviving
at the
Community
College

CHAPTER

5

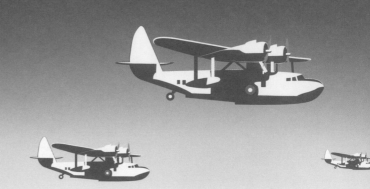

56 How Do I Survive at the Community College?

College survival requires that you perform actions leading to the conditions which enhance college survival. Effectiveness is determined by the behavior we exhibit and the skills we possess. Identifying the behavioral skills which constitute knowing **the system** helps us understand what we have to do to be effective. Knowing and functioning within the system requires a broad range of skills.

Knowing how to access and use **services** will enhance our success in college. Making friends on campus will increase our sense of belonging. **Belonging** is not a skill but a state of mind brought about by the use of effective social skills. **Involvement** in all aspects of academic affairs will influence survival in college. Involvement in college **clubs** produces many benefits such as lifelong friendships, support, leadership skills, project development, and future employment opportunities. **Study Partners** can make the difference between success and failure in a college course.

Using the college **library** is indispensable to academic success for many reasons. It is a place of study, a place to research, and a place to go for assistance. Pursuing **counseling and advisement** will help prevent wasted time and energy. A clearly understood educational plan will further your success. Counselors help you address personal, life, and career issues. Knowing the **policies and procedures** of your college will provide you with the framework to resolve a wide range of academic issues. Knowing your professors could be the most important avenue to college success. Their excitement and commitment to the subject matter may influence your attitude about the subject. A **course load** which is not consistent with your interests, abilities, and desires can derail your academic success. The size and mix of your course load will influence your performance.

The **location** of your college may be an important consideration because it will influence your life as a student. Become familiar with the **resources** on your campus. Accessing resources skillfully is essential in fulfilling your academic needs. Doing the **work** required in your courses is essential in order to succeed. **Asking questions** is an important learning activity. By asking questions your needs are addressed, and you may acquire the information you need. Knowing your **school calendar** will help you be aware of important events, holidays, exam periods, and other significant dates. Be aware that your **attitude** will influence the people around you as well as influencing your success.

57 What Are the Major Barriers to Academic Success?

The purpose of this exercise is to help you understand the number and range of barriers that interfere with academic success. This text will help you address and resolve many of the issues which stem from these barriers. The following list of barriers to academic success has been compiled from the responses of students taking courses in college success. Check off the barriers which you believe impede your academic success.

Study and Learning Barriers

- ❑ Procrastination
- ❑ Motivation
- ❑ Homework overload
- ❑ General education
- ❑ Concentration
- ❑ Relevance of instruction
- ❑ Keeping focused
- ❑ Asking questions
- ❑ Listening to professor
- ❑ Preparation for college

- ❑ Making yourself study
- ❑ Memorization
- ❑ Getting started on projects
- ❑ Course requirements
- ❑ Professor expectations
- ❑ Subjects and concepts
- ❑ Teaching styles
- ❑ Learning disabilities
- ❑ Spelling
- ❑ Language problems

- ❑ Distractions
- ❑ Lack of student aids
- ❑ Controlling study time
- ❑ Attendance
- ❑ Boredom
- ❑ Lack of interest
- ❑ Sitting in class
- ❑ Place to study
- ❑ Comprehension
- ❑ Test anxiety
- ❑ Other_____

Personal and Physical Barriers

- ❑ Money
- ❑ Stress
- ❑ Turning off TV/radio
- ❑ Anger
- ❑ Self-esteem
- ❑ Impatience
- ❑ Health
- ❑ Sex
- ❑ Child care
- ❑ Fear
- ❑ Hunger
- ❑ Transportation

- ❑ Time
- ❑ Tension
- ❑ Work interference
- ❑ Talking on the phone
- ❑ Staying out late
- ❑ Daydreaming
- ❑ Lack of direction
- ❑ Self-discipline
- ❑ Depression
- ❑ Worry
- ❑ Drowsiness
- ❑ Drugs

- ❑ Lack of confidence
- ❑ Pressure
- ❑ Negative thoughts
- ❑ Feeling alienated
- ❑ Guilt about family
- ❑ Relationships
- ❑ Identity
- ❑ Getting up in the morning
- ❑ Values
- ❑ Pain
- ❑ Fatigue
- ❑ Alcohol
- ❑ Other_____

After you have completed the "barriers" questionnaire, list the barriers you have checked in each category.

If you have more barriers than space allows, use a separate sheet of paper.

Study and Learning	Scale 1-10
Total	

Average Score	

Personal and Physical	Scale 1-10
Total	

Average Score	

Rate:

Now that you have listed your barriers, rate each barrier on a scale of 1-10. A rating of 1 would indicate that this is not a very significant barrier whereas a rating of 10 would indicate great significance.

Calculate:

Calculate an average score for the barriers in each category. If your average score is above 5.0, it is advisable that you meet with your instructor or a college counselor to discuss your barriers. Any barrier which has a score of 7 or above should be discussed with your instructor or counselor.

58 How Can I Be Successful in Mathematics?

The community college is an ideal place to master mathematics. For many students, mathematics is the biggest obstacle in achieving educational goals. If you completed the college prep sequence of mathematics courses in high school, you are well on your way to math success. However, many community college students were not college prep in high school, and did not complete more than a course in elementary algebra in high school. Many community college students have difficulty with basic math. If you fall into the latter category, it is not the time to despair, but time to approach math with a strategy for success. Math requires practice and a commitment to do your homework. You need to figure out your current math level in order to select an appropriate math course. You need to be in the right course for you. Attendance is crucial to your math success; therefore, the scheduling of your math course is important. When you schedule your math course, try to leave an hour open after class to do homework. Do your homework immediately after class when the material is still fresh in your mind and you are less likely to forget important math concepts and operations. It is also possible that help is available after class. Get a tutor if you need one and if one is available. If not, get a study partner and form a study group. Study partners and study groups should focus on completed homework review, not on doing homework. Study partners and groups should focus on where you went wrong with a problem. Remember, it is a good idea to do your homework on your own and then come together with your partner and figure out where you went wrong with any problem. If you are not doing well, consider withdrawing and repeating the course. Know the college withdrawal policy and deadline to withdraw without an "F" appearing on your record.

Surviving Mathematics

Take college math assessment.

Review results with counselor.

Pay careful attention to math schedule.

Allow a study hour after your math class.

Do homework immediately after class.

Find a study partner.

Form a study group.

Find a tutor.

Withdraw and repeat class, if necessary.

 # How Can I Solve Math Problems More Effectively?

Learning math requires patience, persistence, discipline, drill, and practice. Your approach to learning mathematics will significantly affect your success. For instance, when solving math problems, it is important to avoid rushing to a solution. Skipping steps may affect your problem solving and mitigate your success since there is a lot more to math than getting the right answer. Most instructors require that you show your work in order to demonstrate your understanding of the process used to find the answer. When solving math problems, study the examples carefully, match your response as closely as possible, and check the reasonableness of your answer. It is helpful to use visualization when solving word problems, and drawing pictures may also help you understand the scope of the problem. Usually, there are not short-cuts. When solving math problems, know the category and type of problem you are learning and working on, and pay close attention to what you are being asked to solve. Math will help you learn to think logically and systematically.

1122

 How Can I Learn to Study Effectively?

Preparation

Assess Motivation to Study

Motivation is an essential factor in performance but is not easy to assess. You may want to ask yourself the following questions: Am I ready to undertake the demands of an academic program which requires substantial study? How will I get myself ready? How can I motivate myself to study? What are the benefits of study?

Make Studying a Priority

When studying becomes a priority, other activities are less likely to interfere with the process of studying. This will make it easier for you to make a firm commitment to studying. Where does studying fall on your list of priorities? Are your actions consistent with the activities you consider priorities?

Make a Study Schedule

A study schedule is a product of effective time management. Do you have sufficient time to study? If not, which activities interfere with studying? Remember, ineffective time management interferes with effective study.

Select a Place to Study

A consistent place to study helps make study habitual. A place to study makes it easier to get started on study assignments and prevents wasting time deciding where to study. Quick and easy access to your place of study is essential to support your study commitment. Many students use the college library to study because they find it difficult to study at home with the family or in an apartment with roommates. You may have to negotiate with others to help you create a conducive study environment.

Gather Materials and Resources for Study

After you have selected a place for study, it is important to have all the materials and supplies at your disposal. Proper lighting, desk, chair, pens, pencils, paper, dictionary, thesaurus, calculator, erasers, notebooks, pads, binders, recorders, computers, and other reference materials are all essential supplies for the study environment.

Develop Concentration and Avoid Distraction

By increasing your motivation, you can increase your ability to concentrate on a learning task. Concentration cannot be forced. Increasing levels of interest will increase levels of concentration. It is almost impossible to avoid distraction; we must be careful not to allow distractions to derail our efforts. Learn techniques to develop concentration and techniques that mitigate the effects of distraction.

Know Exactly What Is Expected From You In Each Course

Be sure you have the syllabus for each course you take. Carefully read the requirements of the course. Ask your instructor any questions you may have about those requirements. If you find you do not know what is expected, make an appointment with your professor or teaching assistant. Know what is expected early in a course. Do not wait until the midterm exam to find out what is expected.

Develop a Strategy for Each Assignment

Formulate a plan to complete each assignment. Break the assignment into different steps, stages, and phases. This enables you to know where to start, continue and end the assignment. If you don't formulate a strategy, you may be lost and unable to effectively complete the assignment. Without a strategy, you may lack organization and waste valuable time.

Activation

Attend Class

Class attendance is essential in order to perform well in college. If you are not in class, you can acquire the information you need only through secondary sources. You have to be in class in order to get the most out of your learning experience.

Take Notes

Notes are a transcript of material covered in a class lecture. Notes should include the fundamental material of the course being taken. A commitment is essential to effective note-taking. The quality of note-taking can easily determine the level of performance on exams. Note-taking techniques can improve your ability to take notes.

Use Study Techniques, Skills, Strategies, and Procedures

Effective study skills can significantly increase your level of academic performance. It is important that you learn how to learn. Look for ways to increase your study effectiveness. Learn study techniques, strategies, skills, and procedures.

Use Learning Strategies

Learning strategies combine knowledge of how we learn with strategies for effective learning. Underlying a learning strategy is a learning principle. Learning a task can be accomplished through practice, and how that practice is applied is a learning strategy.

Start Early on Assignments

There are many advantages to starting assignments early. The first is to give yourself sufficient time to do the best job. Second, you will alleviate the pressure that accumulates from doing assignments late. And if you run into any difficulties you can get help.

Look For The Value, Relevance, Meaning, and Purpose of Learning

At times it is difficult to recognize the value, relevance, meaning, and purpose of our coursework. Just as you cannot see the beauty of a house when a foundation is being put in, neither can you see the value, relevance, meaning and purpose of your education as you are acquiring it. Learning carries its own purpose, and it is through constant learning that life derives much of its meaning. All learning is relevant if you see the relationship between what you learn and other aspects of living.

Look for Application

For many of us, it is difficult to see the relationship between theory and practice. The application of learning is a vital leap from theory. Look for ways to apply your learning. Ask yourself, "How can I apply this to my daily life?" Application makes learning relevant and gives us confidence in ourselves. Through application of learning, we can change our world.

Make Connections

Recognizing that life is a complex pattern of relationships allows us to construct innumerable meanings. Seeing the connection in our learning gives us great insight and understanding. Seeing how different things are related makes the discovery of learning very exciting.

Keep It Quiet!

A quiet environment is most conducive for study. In all probability any kind of noise, including music, interferes with learning. The more consistently you keep a quiet study environment, the more likely you are to learn to enjoy the quietude.

Maintain Moderate Levels of Anxiety

Too little or too much anxiety interferes with performance. Excessive anxiety interferes with focusing on a task. Low levels of anxiety do not energize you to take on a task. Moderate levels of anxiety keep you alert and focused on the task. Follow study sessions with a reward. Behavior that is rewarded or reinforced is sustained. Study behavior is a type of behavior that students want to maintain and develop. Rewards are pleasant activities, objects, and experiences which we enjoy and give us pleasure. There are many types of rewards, and you must discover what reward is for you.

Learn Actively

Learning is a participatory process which requires your involvement. An active engagement in the learning situation significantly promotes learning. Learning is a dialogue, a conversation between you, your professors and other students. Find ways to express yourself meaningfully in the classroom setting.

Evaluation

Identify Study and Learning Difficulties

Study and learning difficulties are any obstacles that interfere with study and learning. Difficulties in comprehending reading material may be an example of a study or learning difficulty. Learn to identify and describe study and learning difficulties. Examples of study and learning difficulties may fall into the areas of memory, attention, and interest.

What Kind of Learner Are You?

Discover your learning style. Look at your sensory system. Which sense do you favor when you learn? Do you like using your eyes? Ears? Your sense of touch and movement? Your sense of smell? Which of these senses do you combine when you learn best?

Evaluate Study and Learning Effectiveness

Periodically take the time to evaluate how well you are learning and how you are doing in your classes to determine what can be improved. Your grades are one indicator of study and learning effectiveness. You might even consider establishing your own criteria in regard to your academic performance. Examine the things you do well and the things you do not do well. How can you make yourself more efficient and more effective in the things you don't do well?

Support

Seek Help for Study and Learning Difficulties

Most colleges have individuals with expertise in the areas of study and learning problems. Seek help in diagnosing any study or learning problem you think impedes your effectiveness as a student. Many students have study and learning difficulties which are not necessarily considered disabilities.

Consider a Tutor

Having a tutor helps you stay on task and understand the material. Some tutors are trained in specific areas, while others may have a broad range of expertise. An important function of the tutor is to be supportive and help you do the work.

Find a Mentor

Many colleges and universities have mentoring programs. Frequently mentors are individuals who are already working in your chosen field. They can offer you valuable guidance and support. Mentors are valuable role models who demonstrate that it is possible for us to achieve our goals.

Form Study Pairs and Study Groups

Finding just one other person to share your classroom experience may be very helpful. If your study partner helps you to focus on the course tasks, the combined effort may be beneficial. Being completely alone and isolated in a difficult course may readily result in poor performance in that course. A study partner or group helps you bridge the isolation of being a solitary student. Find an individual with whom you can share the pressure that you experience in difficult courses. You and your study partner or study group need to keep in mind that addressing the assignments of a course is the primary function of the study group. Study groups emphasize the discussion of the material to be learned. Others emphasize where individuals go wrong in the solution of problems. This is especially true of math and science study groups. The formation of study pairs and study groups

is a college survival skill which can make the difference between poor and optimum performance in any course.

Attitude

Make an Effort

Anything worth doing requires a conscious effort. Making an effort implies that the mere application of your will power contributes to whether important undertakings are completed. Making an effort means that you try to do your best when given an assignment. In short, making an effort means that you're willing to work.

Have a Positive Attitude

A positive attitude is the natural evolution of believing in yourself and knowing that you can accomplish your goals. A positive attitude is a product of having a hopeful attitude about the future. If you cannot maintain a positive attitude, you may need to address some self-esteem issues.

Cultivate a Strong Belief in Yourself and in Your Abilities

A belief in oneself and one's abilities creates a reservoir of strength that is helpful when any demands are made upon you. Believing in your capacity to do well in specific activities greatly enhances performance and a sense of self-competence. A strong belief in oneself comes from real accomplishments and a strong sense of self-worth.

61 How Do I Identify My Learning Style?

Do you pay attention to the way you learn? Do you know how you learn best? Do you know what type of cues from the environment help or hinder your learning? When you are in a classroom, what type of instruction do you prefer?

Individuals generally can be classified into three categories of learning styles: visual, auditory, and kinesthetic-tactile. Which best fits you? Of course, most of us use all of our senses in learning and in responding to the environment, but we probably have definite preferences.

Visual Learners

Visual learners are prompted to learn more effectively when presented with a series of visual cues. They learn best by seeing and reading. Visual learners frequently prefer to work alone, enjoy conducting research, and like writing about their findings.

Auditory Learners

Auditory learners learn best by listening and hearing. Auditory learners enjoy discussion and interaction and do not enjoy assignments involving substantial reading. Auditory learners like to interact with others and participate in group discussion.

Kinesthetic–Tactile Learners

Kinesthetic-Tactile learners learn best using motor activities. Kinesthetic-Tactile learners enjoy manipulating objects and using various digital movements while learning. Kinesthetic-Tactile learners feel compelled to get up and move about while engaged in learning activities. They enjoy sports and are mechanically inclined.

Knowing, understanding, and using your learning style will help increase your learning effectiveness. The following activities are designed to help you determine your preferred learning style, evaluate your learning style, maximize your learning style, and match your learning style with study techniques.

62 How Can I Determine How I Learn Best?

Check the visual, auditory or kinesthetic-tactile activities which are most characteristic of you.

Visual

❏ I likc reading.
❏ I use pictures, charts and graphs to study.
❏ I prefer written directions.
❏ I remember by taking notes and making lists.
❏ I am good at using maps.
❏ I enjoy reading books, magazines, and newspapers.
❏ I enjoy research and writing.
❏ I enjoy drawing, designing and sketching.
❏ I use mental pictures to remember.
❏ I spell difficult words by writing them down.

Auditory

❏ I remember oral directions.
❏ I read aloud to understand new concepts.
❏ I enjoy listening to music.
❏ I enjoy listening to a lecture or play.
❏ I understand academics better when listening to a lecture or tape.
❏ I like discussion and exchange of ideas.
❏ I remember things people say.
❏ I enjoy hearing foreign languages.
❏ I spell difficult words by sounding them out.
❏ I enjoy listening to books on tape.

Kinesthetic–Tactile

❏ I enjoy working with computers.
❏ I doodle during lectures.
❏ I enjoy sightseeing.
❏ I enjoy contact with others such as hugging and handshaking.
❏ I enjoy dance and movement.
❏ I participate in sports.
❏ I prefer to create and build projects.
❏ I snack, smoke, or chew gum while studying.
❏ I fidget with objects while studying.
❏ I enjoy using machines.

Maximizing Your Learning Style

Maximize your learning style by emphasizing your strengths.
Use the following techniques to increase learning efficiency.

Visual

Read silently

Write directions

Use visual study notes and cards

Underline or highlight in your textbook

Visualize meanings

Auditory

Explain material to others

Use recitation

Use tape recordings

Focus on verbal directions and instructions

Use study pairs and groups

Kinesthetic-Tactile

Write outlines

Make lists and graphs

Take notes

Underline or highlight in your textbooks

Stand or walk while studying

How Can I Understand, Learn, and Remember What I Read?

Study techniques are useful in understanding, remembering, and learning material. Here are some proven techniques. **Quick Survey** will help you acquire an overview of the material to be studied and learned when you glance through the required reading material. **In-Depth Preview** will help you develop a comprehensive overview of the material when you read the first and last sentence of each paragraph. **Skimming** is used to identify and find main ideas by quickly searching for them. **Scanning** is a technique used for understanding main ideas by finding and then learning the main ideas. **Read, Stop, and Recite** is an important study technique designed to help the student learn, understand, and remember the material. **Questioning** enables the student to focus attention and learn the reading material by formulating probing questions about that material. **Recitation** is a powerful study and learning technique requiring the recall of important information which is stated in the student's own words. **Underlining** and **Highlighting** are important study techniques because they force the student to be selective and decide what information should be underlined or highlighted. **Review** consolidates learning by giving the student the necessary practice to learn, remember, and master the material. **Don't Read Past A Word You Are Unable To Define** is a technique which prevents the collapse of understanding material because the student defines all unknown words. **Outlining** is a study and learning technique which allows the student to organize material by using the traditional outline structure. **Terminology** brings attention to the importance of knowing the terms of a particular discipline when the student learns the vocabulary in that discipline.

Combining these techniques will greatly increase your learning efficiency by discovering through trial and error which combination of techniques work best for you. In order for these techniques to be helpful, a sufficient amount of application and practice is necessary. **Read** the steps of each technique, **apply** the technique, and **determine** whether it works for you.

Study techniques to enhance understanding, learning, and remembering:

Quick survey

In-depth preview

Skimming

Scanning

Read-Stop-Recite

Questioning

Recitation

Underlining or Highlighting

Review

Don't read past a word you are not able to define

Outlining

Terminology

Study Techniques

1.   Quick Survey

Quick Survey gives you an overview of the material to be read. Quick Survey may be your first step in approaching a reading assignment. Quick Survey takes only a few minutes.

> *Step 1. –* **Survey**
> Quickly survey material to be read.
>
> *Step 2. –* **Read**
> Table of Contents • Chapter Titles • Subheadings
> Illustrations • Graphs • Charts
> Chapter Summaries

2.   In–Depth Preview

In-Depth Preview gives you a comprehensive overview of the material to be read. This technique will take substantially longer than Quick Survey.

> *Step 1. –* **Read**
> All Headings • Chapter Summaries • Captions
>
> *Step 2. –* **Observe**
> Photos • Illustrations • Maps • Graphics
>
> *Step 3. –* **Read**
> Read first and last sentences of every paragraph.

3.   Skimming

Skimming introduces you to the main ideas of a chapter or a book. Skimming lets you search for main ideas; it is not reading word-for-word. Skimming is useful when locating main ideas in the process of reviewing. Skimming is more in-depth than Quick Survey and more selective than In-Depth Preview.

> *Step 1. –* **Glance**
> Glance over material to be read.
>
> *Step 2. –* **Search**
> Search for the main ideas of the material.
>
> *Step 3. –* **Identify**
> Identify main ideas as quickly as possible.
> Do not focus on one main idea to the exclusion of other important ideas.

4. Scanning

Scanning is a search for a main idea. Once that idea is encountered, you stop and read about the main idea in-depth. The objective of scanning is to identify a specific idea you have set out to find.

Step 1. – **Find**
Find the idea.

Step 2. – **Focus**
Focus on the idea.

Step 3. – **Learn**
Learn the idea.

---

5. Read, Stop, Recite

Read, Stop, and Recite is a study technique requiring you to recall and put into your own words what you have just read. Many educators consider Read, Stop and Recite the most important study technique available.

Step 1. – **Read**
Read a small amount of material.

Step 2. – **Stop**
Stop and think about the material you have just read.

Step 3. – **Recite**
Recite or write in your own words what you have just read.

---

6. Questioning

Questioning allows you to focus your attention on specific information you are looking for while reading. The questioning process starts by reading the chapter title. As you read through a chapter you will be questioning the material. Questioning the material facilitates understanding and remembering the material.

Step 1. – **Turn**
Turn chapter title and all subheadings into questions.

Step 2. – **Focus**
Focus your attention on looking for the answers to the questions you have formulated.

Step 3. – **Write**
Write the answer to the questions you have formulated.

Step 4. – **Go Back**
Go Back and find the answers if you cannot answer the questions formulated.

---

7.   Recitation

Recitation is a technique emphasizing the verbalization of material to be learned. Recitation facilitates memorization and learning and is a form of self-testing. Recitation is a powerful study and learning technique requiring the recall of important information stated in your own words. Rather than go back and read a chapter a second or third time, go back and use recitation. Increase the percentage of time reciting the material compared to reading the material.

Step 1. – **Recite**
Recite answers to questions, definitions and facts.
Recite everything to be remembered.

Step 2. – **Explain**
Explain out loud important ideas and theories
to be learned from material studied.

---

8.   Underlining or Highlighting

Underlining or highlighting are study techniques requiring you to identify and decide on the most important ideas and underline or highlight them. Most students underline or highlight too much, indicating a lack of selectivity. Effective underlining or highlighting reduces the size of your memorization task.

Step 1. – **Identify**
Identify the most important ideas in
the material you are studying.

Step 2. – **Decide**
Decide what is the most important idea
on a page, and underline or highlight it.

---

9.   Review

Review is the use of additional attempts to learn, remember, and master the material. The purpose of review is to consolidate, check and test, learn and re-learn, and process previously studied material into long term memory. Without review you may quickly forget the material you are trying to remember. Review is an extremely important technique enabling you to learn and commit material to memory. Study schedules should include specific sessions for review. Brief review periods can be very selective.

Step 1. – **Go Back**
Go back to previously studied material and identify gaps in
your understanding and memory of the material.

Step 2. – **Use Memory Techniques**
Use memory techniques to help you recall and learn the material.

Step 3. – **Re-Read Lecture Notes**
Continued Next Page
Determine if they are complete and accurate. Identify gaps in
learning, understanding, and remembering.

Step 4. – **Re-Read Required Reading Material Notes**
Determine what is essential for you to learn and remember. Use cues
provided in lecture as to essential material to be learned and remembered.

Step 5. – **Recite**
Recite again the essential material to be learned and remembered.

Step 6. – **Re-Organize**
Re-organize material to be learned and remembered.

Step 7. – **Use New Perspective**
As you review study material, attempt to see different patterns,
relationships, details, and new connections between the parts to
the whole, or anything that gives you a new perspective on the material.

Step 8. – **Self-Test**
Test your knowledge and recall of the material by using the question
and answer study format. This will help you determine whether information
has been processed into long-term memory.

10.   Don't Read Past A Word You Are Not Able To Define!

Don't read past a word you are unable to define; look it up in the dictionary! When you read past a word you cannot define, your understanding of the material begins to collapse. The greater the number of words that you cannot define and that you read past, the greater the number of holes in your understanding. Some educators believe this is the most significant study breakdown.

Step 1. – **Stop**
Don't read past a word you cannot define.

Step 2. – **Pause**
Try to determine the meanings of words by using context clues.

Step 3. – **Use the Dictionary!**
Place supporting details under sub-topics.
Supporting details are given as number symbols.

11. Outlining

Outlining is a versatile study technique. You can outline a chapter, term paper, speech, lecture notes, and even a book. Outlining is also an organizing technique. Outlining gives order and structure to ideas. Outlining illustrates the relationship between parts to the whole and shows how ideas are inter-related.

Step 1. – **Identify Major Topics**
Use Roman numerals to place each major topic into sequential order.

Step 2. – **Identify Sub-topics**
Place sub-topics under appropriate major topics. Sub-topics are usually assigned capital letters.

Step 3. – **Identify Supporting Details**
Place supporting details under sub-topics. Supporting details are given as number symbols.

Step 4. – **Identify Details of Supporting Details**
Place details under appropriate supporting details. Use a lower caseletter to identify the detail.

---

12. Terminology

Step 1. – **Organization of Terminology**
Determine how the terminology is organized in your textbook. Some texts may incorporate a glossary. Many texts definethe terms as they appear in the text.

Step 2. – **Listen to Instructor**
Listen to the instructor for correct pronunciation of subject terms.

Step 3. – **Subject Dictionary**
Look for a dictionary on your particular subject. Not all subjects may have this available.

Step 4. – **Learn the Terms**
Use study, learning, and memory techniques to learn the terminology.

Step 5. – **Index Cards**
Consider using index cards to collect and define terms.

Matching Learning Styles and Study Techniques

Increase your learning effectiveness by matching the technique to your learning style.

Visual	Auditory	Kinesthetic–Tactile
Quick Survey	Quick Survey (out loud)	Questioning
In-Depth Preview	In-Depth Preview (out loud)	Underlining
Skimming	Read, Stop, Recite	Outlining
Scanning	Questioning	Terminology
Read, Stop, Recite	Recitation	
Questioning	Review	
Underlining	Terminology	
Review		
Don't Read Past A Word You Are Not Able To Define.		
Terminology		

How Can I Facilitate the Learning Process?

A learning skill is a method, principle, or procedure that facilitates the learning process. Learning skills are associated with learning principles. The conscious application of a learning principle which facilitates learning is a learning skill. Knowledge of how we learn allows us to consciously apply principles of effective learning. Study skills facilitate the learning process without the learner being conscious of the learning principle which underlies learning. For example, reviewing is a study skill, but there are several learning principles that underlie reviewing. The learning principles that underlie reviewing fall within the categories of cognitive learning and information processing. Knowledge and application of these learning principles result in a learning skill.

Enhance learning through:

Practice

Trial and Error

Knowledge of Results

Spaced Practice

Reinforcement and Reward

Cognitive Learning

Modeling

All Your Senses

Staying on Task

Application of Effort

Effortless Effort

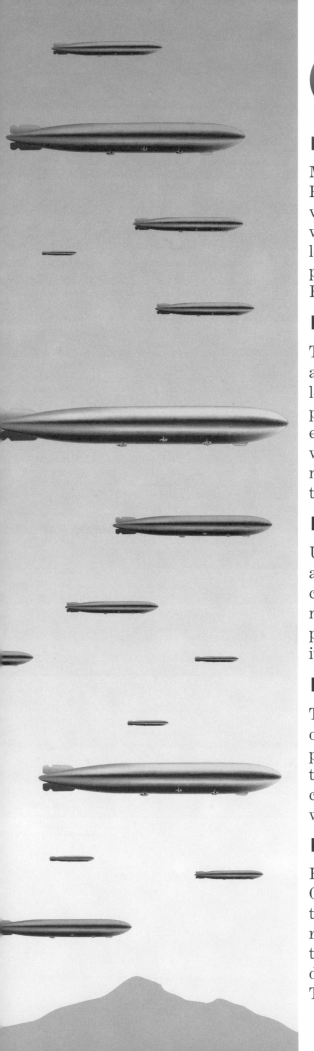

65   What Are Learning Skills?

Learning Skill 1   Practice

Most learning activities can be mastered through practice. Practice seems so obvious that we frequently fail to see its value. Through practice, we learn to solve algebraic equations, write research papers, and give effective speeches. Just as we learn to hit a powerful topspin backhand shot in tennis through practice, we master academic activities through practice. Repetition and review are techniques of practice.

Learning Skill 2   Knowledge of Results

The information that we gain regarding our performance on a learning task provides us with knowledge of effective and less effective responses. All the comments made on a research paper give us valuable information on how to write a more effect research paper. Knowledge of test results tells us what we can do to make more effective and correct responses. We need knowledge of where we go astray in order to get back on target.

Learning Skill 3   All Your Senses

Using all of your senses greatly enhances your ability to learn and remember material. When the senses are all used in combination, we strengthen our ability to remember. Each modality has its own memory sense. Many of us favor a particular sensory modality. If you want to remember it: see it, hear it, say it, feel it, and act on it.

Learning Skill 4   Staying on Task

The ability to stay focused on a task for an extended period of time is difficult for many. Yet many learning tasks require patient and persistent effort. It is the completion of learning tasks that gets us through a course and eventually through college. Frequently, the more task oriented we are, the more we are able to succeed.

Learning Skills 5   Application of Effort

Effort is a conscious attempt to do our best at learning a task. Getting ready to learn isn't always automatic. Effort is easiest to apply when we are motivated to learn. Most learning tasks require a conscious decision to do it. At times effort means that we compel ourselves to act through internal pressure and demands. If you don't give it a try, you may not ever learn it. Trying is making the effort.

Learning Skills 6   Effortless Effort

The more we perform learning tasks, the more automatic and spontaneous our energy. You do it effectively without being conscious of how you do it. Although you have been trained and skilled in writing essays, through effortless effort, you write a great essay without being conscious of how you did it. Your level of functioning becomes more effective and spontaneous.

Learning Skill 7   Spaced Practice

Through spaced practice we learn more in the same amount of time than through time that has been massed together. Two one-half hour study sessions can be much more effective than a one-hour session. Studying a little seven days a week is more effective than extended study two days a week. Short study periods can be effective.

Learning Skill 8   Trial and Error

We learn from our mistakes. We should expect to make mistakes and should be discouraged by them. Our mistakes are a demonstration of knowledge of results. Mistakes tell us something about what we need to do and not do. Trials are further attempts at mastering a task. Sustaining trials requires motivation and effort.

Learning Skill 9   Modeling

We learn from the actions of others. Others learn from our actions. Modeling is a powerful form of learning. Mentors become valuable partners in learning because they become our models. We learn and teach through example. You can model the positive behavior you see in others, and you can also model the negative behavior you see in others. Be watchful and attentive of what is modeled around you.

Learning Skill 10   Reinforcement and Reward

Behavior that is reinforced or rewarded is strengthened. Behaviors that are strengthened tend to be repeated. Behavior is governed by its consequences. Study and learning behaviors must be reinforced in order to be sustained.

Learning Skill 11   Cognitive Learning

The learning activities of the brain are very complex. We learn and solve problems through complex mental operations. As human beings, we have a tremendous thinking capacity. We learn through our cognitive processes. The mental and intellectual activity of the mind appears to have no limit.

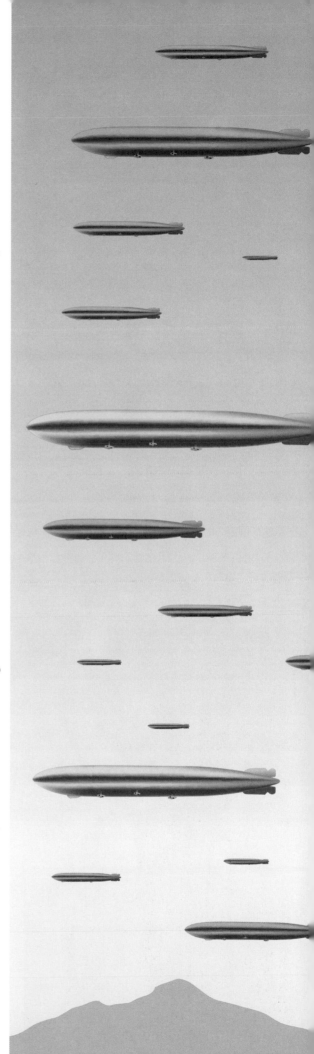

147

66 What Is the Note–Taking Process?

Note-Taking gives us a written transcript of facts, opinions, ideas, theories, and information presented in an academic course of study enabling the student to learn the material. This transcript is used for organizing, processing and remembering, and reviewing material at a later date.

Observation initiates the note-taking process. Many learning situations start with observation. Observation is the conscious and unconscious use of our sensory system to acquire and process information. Observation allows you to access verbal and non-verbal information from the learning situation. Observation allows you to understand important concepts which are presented through demonstration. Observation is one of the primary methods by which we accumulate vast amounts of information and draw conclusions.

Listening actively to class lectures provides the basis for effective note-taking. Listening means paying careful attention to the content of the class lecture. Knowing what to listen for is central to the note-taking process. There are many signals and cues that alert the note-taker to the importance, order, and structure of ideas presented. Frequently, instructors will give a topic to their lecture, identify issues and problems to be presented, identify a time span to be covered, present a formula, and introduce problem solving methods and procedures. By listening actively, you will be able to determine the content, structure, and importance of ideas presented in class lecture.

Processing and sorting material as presented in lecture is an important part of learning. Students are not merely recording what is being presented but actively thinking, analyzing, reflecting, and processing information while it is being presented. When great quantities of material are presented, the student needs to sort out what is important. By carefully processing and sorting information, students are able to reduce the amount of information necessary to record in note-taking.

Writing quickly and legibly increases the usability of your notes. Writing quickly allows you to keep up with the lecture. Selecting appropriate and comfortable tools will help you with quick writing.

Formats for note-taking help organize ideas. This helps you understand the structure of ideas presented in lecture. Some note-taking formats include:

- Outlining
- Short Paragraphs
- Key Word
- Short Phrase
- Mapping
- Margin and Page Formatting

Examine and revise your notes the same day. Are your notes usable and legible? If not, this is the time to examine your notes and determine if they need to be re-written. If you find gaps and incomplete ideas, you may have to first revise, then re-write your notes. By examining and revising the same day, it will be easier to remember what was presented in class lecture. Examining, revising, and re-writing all contribute to the understanding of class lecture. These procedures provide valuable repetition and the means to remember important material.

Compare and discuss your notes with another member of the class. This becomes an additional method for learning class material, and it allows you to find gaps in your transcript of the lecture. Comparing and discussing your notes with another member of the class provides another valuable step in the learning process.

Guidelines for Note–Taking

1. Assess Motivation

Taking effective notes requires both motivation and skill. Are you motivated to take notes and learn the skills of note-taking?

2. Assess Note–Taking Needs of Each Course

Most courses are structured around a combination of lectures and readings. Some courses are structured around the required readings, others are structured around lectures. Courses which rely heavily on lecture require more note-taking. Your notes then will be an important source of test preparation.

3. Preparation

Make sure you come to class with necessary supplies such as paper, pencils, pens, erasers, notebooks, required readings and books, calculators and any other supplies specified by the instructor.

4. Note-Taking Format

There are several note-taking formats such as short paragraphing, outlining, mapping, short phrasing, margin and page formatting, and key word method. Choose the format that works best for you and your classes.

5. Notes Verbatim

Avoid trying to take word-for-word notes. You will soon tire and not be able to keep up with the lecture.

6. Selection

Make yourself decide what is important, and write it down.

7. Develop Your Own Shorthand

Develop your own shorthand, and maintain a key to your abbreviations. For example, environment may be abbreviated "evt." And psychology, "psy."

67 How Can I Keep Up with Note-Taking?

Observe

Take in as much as you can as fast as you can.

Listen

Listen for the essentials

Think

Think about the main ideas

Write

Write quickly and get down the supporting details.

68 How Can I Improve Test Performance?

Test-taking is an integral part of academic life. It is through effective test-taking that we achieve academic success. Since grades are seen as important in society, we are pressured into competing and pursuing high marks. We need to recognize the importance of grades because they are used as criteria for completion of academic programs, entrance into graduate and professional schools, scholarships, employment opportunities, and the grades you receive on tests are frequently seen as measures of competence and ability.

Test Performance

Students frequently use grades as measures of self-worth and intelligence. Consequently, there doesn't seem to be any college event more threatening to a student's self-worth than test-taking. Poor performance on tests can be devastating to students for many reasons and can easily lead to catastrophic thinking: "If I do poorly on tests, I am worthless. If I do poorly on tests, I am dumb. If I do poorly on tests, I will never succeed." This type of thinking contributes to a poor sense of self-worth, fear and test anxiety.

Improving Test Performance

Since grades are important and are largely the products of test-taking, it is important to perform well on tests. Many ways exist to improve performance on tests: preparation, practice, prediction, memory techniques, relaxation techniques, self-testing, study pairs and groups, time management, and using available resources. The most obvious and immediate method for improving test performance is practice. Through practice, you will become a better test-taker. The application of practice in taking tests and mastering material for tests will increase your test performance. Practice is an essential part of preparation, and there is no substitute for preparation in order to improve test performance. If we expect to do well on exams, we must do the necessary preparation.

151

Memory Techniques

Good test performance relies heavily on the ability to retrieve information from long-term memory. Have you learned the material so that you can remember the information during the test? Using various strategies to encode information into long-term memory should aid with retrieving the information during the test. Effective use of memory techniques will improve test performance. With review, you are more likely to remember important material that will appear on tests. Frequent reviews will help you deep-process information needed for exams. Self-testing is an excellent test preparation technique. Creating and taking your own exam will help you when you take the course exam. Self-testing provides valuable review and practice. Using pairs and groups can be helpful for exam preparation. Explaining course material to others and being questioned by others regarding course material provides important recitation and practice which aids learning and memory.

Prediction

A major technique used in preparing for exams is prediction. Predicting what will be on an exam will help with your preparation. With practice you will be able to predict a high percentage of the questions that will appear on exams. Determining the main concepts and ideas covered in a course should aid in your prediction and preparation for exams. Occasionally, professors will indicate what will be on a test, and you need to learn that specified material well. "Knowing that you know" the content material of course should do much to alleviate anxiety and ensure good test performance. You can increase your sense of "knowing that you know" through review, practice, and overlearning.

Test–Taking Perspective

If you find that you are having significant test-taking difficulties, you may need to take advantage of services offered by your school. You may need to obtain a tutor, learn relaxation techniques, test-taking strategies and memory techniques. Keep a proper perspective on tests. Remember that tests are not a measure of your worth. Tests of course content do not measure intelligence, frequently do not test what they are supposed to test, and can be culturally biased. Guard against catastrophic thinking and learn to relax when it comes to test-taking.

Improve test performance through:

Preparation

Practice

Prediction

Memory Techniques

Relaxation Techniques

Self-Testing

Study Partners

Study Groups

Time Management

Resources

69 | What Techniques Can I Use for Taking Exams?

Exam Procedures

Read test instructions. Pay close attention to what you are being asked to do.

Review the entire test and determine the assigned value of each item.

Time yourself. Decide how much time you are going to devote to each test item.

Do easy items first and go back to difficult items later.

Complete all items. Do not leave any items blank.

Guess when you don't know.

Check your response for each test item.

Essay Exams

Read the instructions. Pay attention to key words which describe what you are being asked to do. Manage time so you can complete all questions.

Organize your thoughts. Before you begin to write your answer to an essay question think through your answer.

Write ideas and structure them before you begin writing the essay.

Respond to the question and keep focused.

Include main points for which instructor may be looking.

Proofread your essay response.

Multiple Choice Exams

Read the question carefully. What are you being asked to do?

Be alert to "all of the above" and "none of the above" response alternatives.

Be prepared to make fine discriminations. The more precise the discrimination between responses, the more difficult it is to make the correct response.

Read each of the given answers and initiate a process of elimination. If you don't know the correct response, increase your odds of making the correct response through the process of elimination.

Select study strategies. The careful selection of study strategies can increase your ability to recognize correct responses on a multiple choice exam.

70 How Do I Manage Test Anxiety?

Prepare

Go into the test situation well prepared. The more confident you feel about having mastered the material for the test, the less likely you are to become anxious.

Overlearn

Once you have mastered the material, continue learning the material beyond your previous level of mastery.

Relax

Use the relaxation techniques outlined in this book. Attempt to cultivate an alert and relaxed response to testing situations. You want to replace anxiety with an alert, relaxed response.

Don't Catastrophize

Catastrophic thinking follows this pattern: "If I fail this exam, I will fail this course. If I fail this course, my grade point average will go down. If my grade point average goes down, then I will not be able to get into graduate school. If I can't get into graduate school, I will not become a professional. If I don't become a professional, then others will think that I'm not worthy. If others think I'm not worthy, then I will be unlovable. If I'm not loved, then I will be miserable the rest of my life." Avoid falling into this trap.

Use Imagery of Success

Imagine yourself in the testing situation feeling alert and relaxed. You are completing each test item with a high degree of confidence. You feel excited but not anxious. You see yourself making correct responses on the exam and ultimately receiving back the exam with an A+ at the top of your paper.

Use Awareness Practice

Notice where your attention is focused. Awareness of anxiety frequently reduces anxiety. Awareness of your responses frequently helps you control your responses.

Learn Test–Taking Techniques

The more test-taking techniques you know, the less anxious you may feel when confronted with a test-taking situation. Knowing how to take a test helps alleviate anxiety. Test-taking techniques tend to increase self-confidence and reduce anxiety.

Tests Do Not Measure Your Worth

A test is not a measure of your worth. Always combat feeling inadequate when you perform poorly on an exam. A test is not the measure of a person. A test result is usually a particular score on a specific day for a specific test.

71   How Can I Increase My Ability to Remember?

Human beings are very complex information processors. We are bombarded with vast quantities of information of which only a fraction is processed. We pay attention to and recognize only a small amount of information which comes from the environment. Memory, like all other psychological processes, cannot be directly observed. Therefore, models have been developed which are attempts to explain the complex functions of memory. Information processing theorists who study how humans encode, store, process and retrieve information use flow charts to describe and represent these complex functions of human memory. Flow charts are graphic representations used to illustrate the complex functions of memory.

Memory Stores

Many memory theorists assume that we have three memory stores, each of which holds different amounts of information and for different periods of time. These memory stores are called sensory register (SR), short-term memory (STM), and long-term memory (LTM).

The sensory register is considered very brief and registers information from the environment in its original form. Sensory register lasts about four seconds. Short-term memory holds a limited amount of information for a short period of time. Short-term memory holds about seven bits of information for about fifteen seconds. Unlike sensory register and short-term memory, long-term memory can hold vast quantities of information for a lifetime.

Many memory theorists believe that information stored in long-term memory is permanent. Not only is the information permanent, but we seem to have unlimited capacity to store information. Information that reaches long-term memory has been encoded by mechanisms which have facilitated the storage of that information.

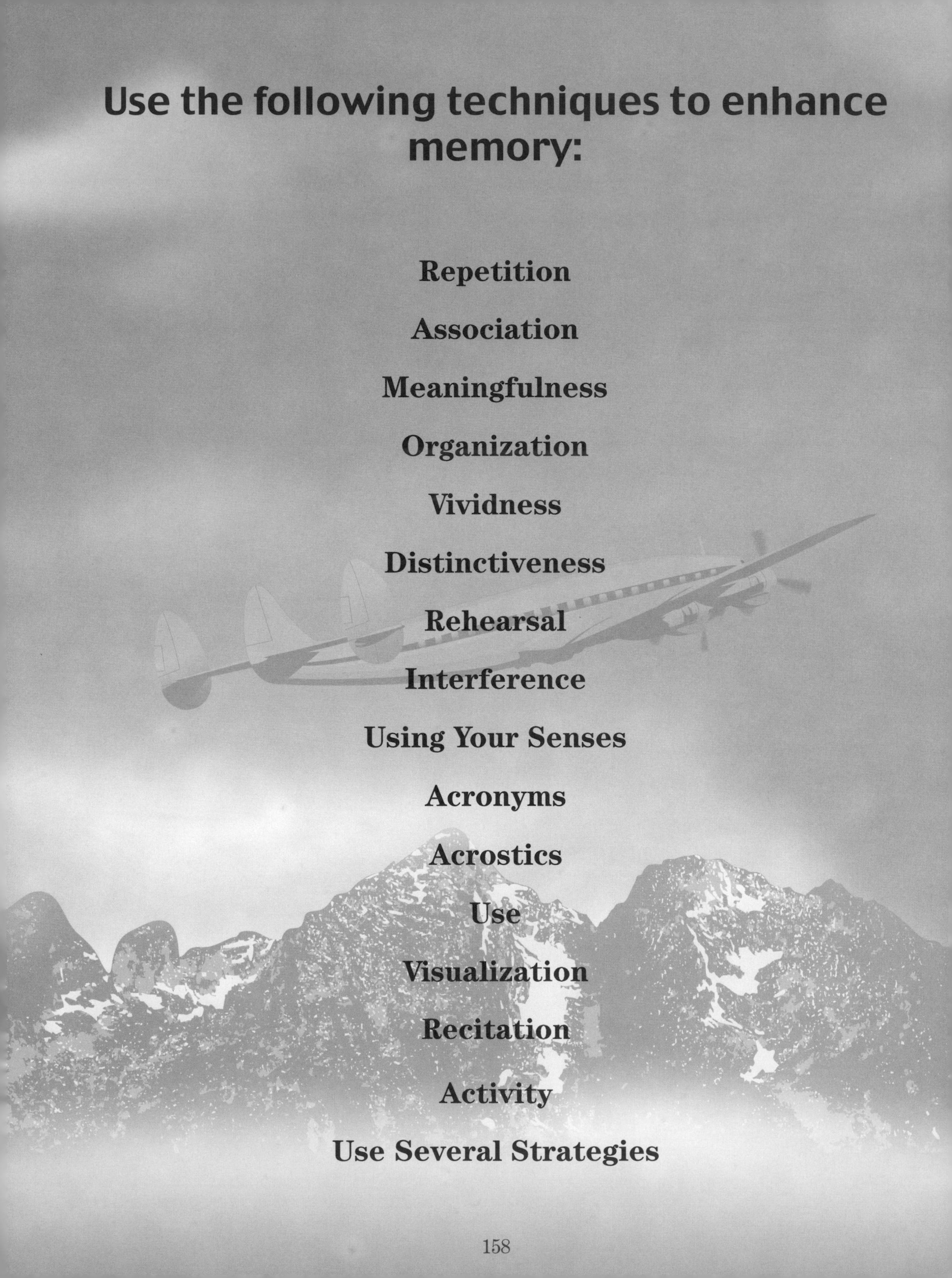

Use the following techniques to enhance memory:

Repetition

Association

Meaningfulness

Organization

Vividness

Distinctiveness

Rehearsal

Interference

Using Your Senses

Acronyms

Acrostics

Use

Visualization

Recitation

Activity

Use Several Strategies

72 What Are Memory Techniques?

1. Repetition

Repetition is immediate and easy to use. We can rely on repetition to hold information in short-term memory by simply repeating information verbally and mentally. We can hold on to it for a longer period of time through repetition which allows for the maintenance of information in short-term memory and creates the possibility for further processing. Repetition may create different patterns and sensory impressions, which may add additional meaning and therefore allow for further processing of information.

2. Association

Associating a new idea with an old idea may be one of the easiest ways to remember the new idea. Associations make connections of new information with stored information creating possibilities for deeper processing of information. Associations create patterns which may introduce and therefore facilitate further processing of information.

3. Meaningfulness

Meaningfulness may be one of the most powerful encoding mechanisms for processing new information into long-term memory. Meaningfulness relates new information to stored information in long-term memory and allows us to encode information.

4. Organization

Organizing information into meaningful patterns helps us process and remember the information. Chunks of information which contain little meaning can be organized into clumps of information which do have meaning. New clumps can reduce the number of chunks to remember, and the new clumps may give us cues to remember other clumps.

5. Vividness

Chunks of information that are vividly encoded are more memorable thank chunks that do not get our attention. Attention is captured by size, color, intensity, novelty, and unexpectedness.

6. Distinctiveness

By concentrating on distinctiveness of information, we can remember it with greater ease. For example, when studying a foreign language noticing the distinctive features of words can help you remember the vocabulary. Some foreign language words offer very few cues that help us remember them. By noticing the distinctive features, you can begin to notice patterns which will further assist in learning vocabulary.

7. Rehearsal

Rehearsal is a type of repetition. There are two types of rehearsal: maintenance and elaborative. Maintenance rehearsal is used to holds bits of information in short-term memory. Holding a phone number in short-term memory until it is used is a type of maintenance rehearsal. The repetition used to remember a complicated speech is an example of elaborative rehearsal. In this type of rehearsal, you used stored information to help remember your speech. You relate the new speech to previously learned speeches, famous speakers, and memories triggered by the new speech.

8. Interference

Learning new information is interfered with what has been previously learned. Learning new information also interferes with the remembering of old information. Learning situations produce both types of interferences. These interferences obstruct the acquisition of new information, and the retrieval of old information.

9. Using Your Senses

Using various combinations of your sensory system, hearing, seeing, touching, smelling, and tasting facilitate remembering information. Each sense possesses its own memory system. We can remember the sound of an old song, the smell of flowers, the taste of an old favorite dish, and the touch and sight of an old friend.

10. Acronyms

Acronyms are usually formed by taking the first letter of a series of items to be remembered and forming a word. Acronyms need not always form a recognizable word. Acronyms help in both the storage and retrieval of information. Acronyms are very useful in organizing random bits of information into meaningful clumps of information. For example, the acronym HOMES is very useful in remembering the Great Lakes. Huron, Ontario, Michigan, Erie, and Superior.

11. Acrostics

Acrostics are similar to acronyms in that they both use letters and position of letters to provide cues to remember more complicated information. Acrostics use the first letter of words in a phrase or sentence to act as cues for the retrieval of information.

12. Use

Use contributes to the remembering of information. Using information helps with the retrieval of information.

13. Visualization

Forming mental images of information we want to remember helps in the processing, storage, and retrieval of the information. Visualizations which catch our attention by size, inappropriateness, exaggeration, and ridiculousness help us remember information. Visualization allows us to use more of our brain.

14. Recitation

When you study, it is a good idea to recite everything you need to remember. Say it aloud in your own words. Reciting information through verbal expression helps in processing information. When you recite information, you pay attention to it. Attending to information helps process information.

15. Activity

Actively discussing information helps in making it memorable. Walking slowly as you read may enhance remembering material. Standing as you study can help in the retention of information.

16. Use Several Strategies

By combining memory techniques, you can process information in a variety of ways which helps in the retrieval of information.

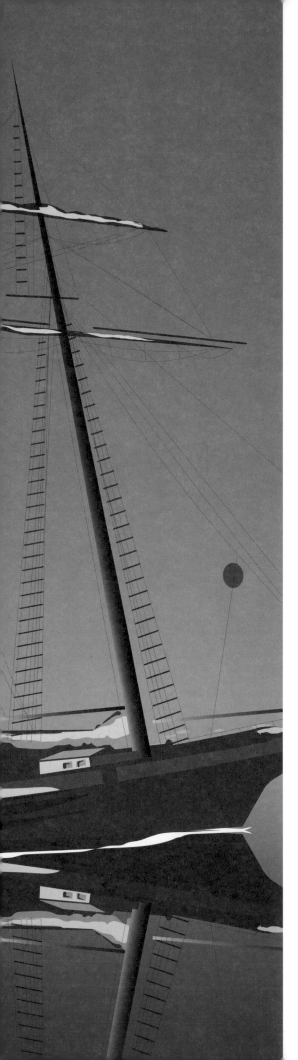

73 What Is the Writing Process?

Anyone can write. If you have something to say, you can write. The primary purpose of writing is to communicate. Everything else in the process is subordinate to that purpose. Writing consists of several different activities, stages, phases, or steps. The stages consist of pre-writing, organizing, writing a rough draft, revising and editing and proof-reading. These activities are repeatable and through practice you increase your skill in doing these activities. The various stages of writing can help you concentrate on one activity at a time. Knowing the specific tasks of each stage helps you identify where you are in the writing process.

Pre–Writing

In the initial stage of writing, it is helpful to abandon perfectionistic demands and pressures of needing to be correct and accurate in your writing. Let go of the censor in your head. Most of us have this censor which makes excessive demands to perform perfectly on writing projects. One of the most effective techniques for letting go of the "censor," or "critical parent," as you write is free writing. Free writing consists of allowing a free flow of ideas without censorship and recording them as they emerge. Free writing is a powerful technique for getting started and working through a writer's block.

Organizing

Organizing the products of your pre-writing activities should help yield a limited and focused topic, a thesis statement, and a rough outline of your writing project. The thesis statement allows the reader to know what the paper is about. A thesis statement is sometimes controversial and gives some indication of what you want your audience to understand, and reveals your opinion and position on a topic. It is the central organizing idea of your paper.

162

Writing a Rough Draft

You can begin writing your rough draft by using free writing. After you have written several paragraphs, you can compare the contents of these paragraphs with your outline. If you get stuck and your free writing does not yield additional material, examine the main ideas that you may want to develop. You may be able to develop your rough draft by adhering to your outline. Some find this difficult. As long as you can sustain your writing, you will have something to work on. A blank sheet of paper gives you nothing to work with. As you write your rough draft, you can repeatedly ask yourself if you are writing to your outline and thesis. It is also possible to write a paper without a rough outline but not recommended. You can generate many paragraphs through free-writing and later examine the content of those paragraphs, and then write an outline.

Revising

After completing your rough draft, you can start with the revision process. Most writers believe that revision is the most critical stage of writing. Many writers spend more time on revision that any other writing activity. When you revise, you re-think, re-examine, re-interpret, re-analyze, and re-construct arguments, presuppositions, logic, conclusions, and implications incorporated in your first draft. Some writers will revise a paper several times. Revision frequently includes major changes to a paper.

Editing

Editing is the phase in the writing process where the primary focus is the accuracy of your writing. In the editing phase, you examine your grammar and sentence structure. The other major function of editing is to examine your writing style. Is your style appropriate for your audience? When you examine the correctness of your sentences, your first concern should be whether you have written complete sentences. When you edit you should be concerned about

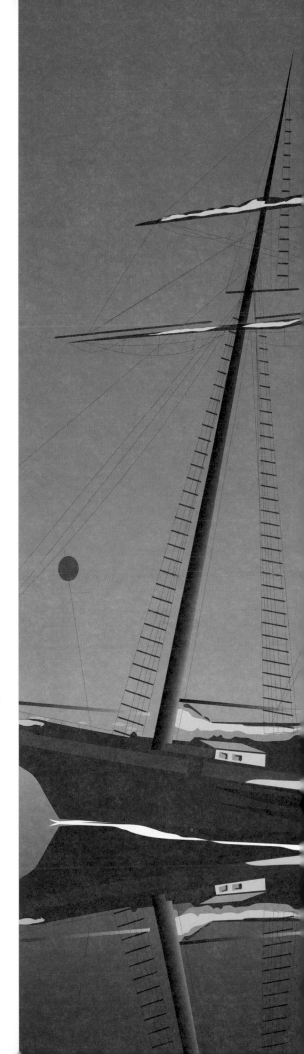

the following: complete sentences, subject-verb agreement, pronoun antecedent agreement, and avoid fragments, comma splices, run-ons and dangling phrases. Editing initiates closure to the writing process of the first draft. It does not involve major revisions. If you are dissatisfied with your first draft, you may need to go back rewrite, revise, and develop a second draft, and initiate the editing process again.

Proofreading

Proofreading is the last function of the writing process. In this phase you are no longer concerned with making major changes to your work. The focus of proofreading is to insure correct punctuation, capitalization, and spelling. Proofreading is not an additional examination of the content of your work.

Summary

As described previously, the writing process consists of several definable activities: pre-writing, organizing, writing a first draft, revision, editing, and proofreading. All writers seem to employ these major activities of the writing process, but not all writers strictly adhere to any proper reference of writing. Several of the writing activities can be done simultaneously. Some writers edit and proof immediately after writing or while writing. It is your task to discover how you best engage in the various activities of writing. There is no set formula for writing, although writing seems to consist of several definable activities.

74 What Is Critical Thinking?

Asking Questions

Asking probing questions is an important step toward thinking critically. Many students are hesitant to ask questions in a classroom environment. Many students fail to ask questions because they fear how they may appear to others. Other students may have difficulty formulating questions. The ability to question what you are learning is an important step in learning and thinking more critically.

Conversation

Asking questions is one way we can engage in the learning process. An additional way is to engage the instructor and other students in conversations about issues which are thought-provoking and require critical thinking. Learning to think critically through conversation and participation is the substance of learning. Many students fail to participate in the conversation because they feel that what they have to say is not important or relevant. Others think they are not capable of being intellectual or do not desire to be so. Anyone who enjoys ideas is an intellectual. Many students need to be encouraged to use their abilities to think and participate with others.

Intellectual standards that apply to thinking in every subject:

Clear	Unclear
Precise	Imprecise
Accurate	Inaccurate
Relevant	Irrelevant
Consistent	Inconsistent
Logical	Illogical
Deep	Superficial
Complete	Incomplete
Significant	Trivial
Adequate	Inadequate
Fair	Prejudicial

Reference: 12th International Conference on Critical Thinking

75 How Do I Cite Articles from Databases?

(MLA Style)

Journal article format for the "Works Cited" page.

Author, Name. "Title of the Article." <u>Name of the Journal</u> Volume number.issue number (year) : page numbers. <u>Name of the Electronic Database</u>. Library Name, City, State. Date article was viewed <web address of database>.

Magazine article format for the "Works Cited" page.

Author, Name. "Title of the Article." <u>Name of the Magazine</u> day Month year published: Page numbers. <u>Name of the Electronic Database</u>. Library Name, City, State. Date Article was viewed <web address of database>.

SAMPLE CITATIONS

CQ Researcher

Clark, Charles S. "The FBI Under Fire." <u>CQ Researcher</u> 7.4 (April 11, 1997) <u>CQ Researcher</u>. Oxnard College Library, Oxnard, CA 16 Jan. 2003 <u>http://enw.softlineweb.com.</u>

Ethnic NewsWatch (sample citation for a **magazine article**)

Flores, Angelique. "Media Mergers May Pose Problems for Hispanics." <u>Hispanic</u> 30 Nov. 2002: 44. <u>Ethnic NewsWatch.</u> Oxnard College Library, Oxnard, CA. 16 Jan. 2003 <u>http://enw.softlineweb.com.</u>

FACTS.com

"Safe Drinking Water Act Signed." <u>Facts On File World News Digest</u> 22 August 1996. <u>FACTS.com</u>. Oxnard College Library, Oxnard, CA. 16 Jan. 2003 <u>http://www.2facts.com/.</u>

Health and Wellness Resource Center

(sample citation for an article from a reference **book)**

Jacobs, J. Todd. "Prevention of Sexuality Transmitted Diseases." <u>Clinical Reference Systems</u>. Broomfield, CO: McKesson HBOC, 2001, <u>Health and Wellness Resource Center.</u> Oxnard College Library, Oxnard, CA. 16 Jan. 2003 <http://web2.infortrac.galegroup.com>.

(sample citation for a **journal article**)

Parker, Richard A. "A 45-Year Old Woman with Obsessive-Compulsive Disorder: One Year Later." <u>JAMA</u> 287.8 (2002): 1037. <u>Health and Wellness Resource Center</u>. Oxnard College Library, Oxnard, CA. 16 Jan. 2003 <u>http://web2.infotrac.galegroup.com.</u>

ProQuest (sample citation for a **newspaper article**)

Stevenson, Richard W. "Bush Urges Congress to Extend Welfare Law, with Changes." <u>New York Times</u> 15 Jan. 2003, East Coast late ed.: A18. <u>ProQuest</u>. Oxnard College Library, Oxnard, CA. 16 Jan. 2003 <u>http://proquest.com.</u>

Sources: Gibaldi, J. MLA Handbook for Writers of Research Papers (1999) and Using Modern Language Association (MLA) Format,
Purdue UniversityOnline Writing Lab <u>*http://owl.english.purdue.edu/handouts/research/r_mla.html*</u>
Prepared by T. Stough & H. Rodriguez, Fall 2003. OCLIB

(APA Style)

CQ Researcher

Clark, C.S. (1997, April 11). The FBI under fire. <u>CQ Researcher</u>, 7(4). Retreived January 16, 2003, from CQ Researcher.

Ethnic NewsWatch (sample citation for a **magazine article**)

Flores, A. (2002, November 30). Media mergers may pose problems for Hispanics. <u>Hispanic</u>, 44. Retrieved January 16, 2003, from Ethnic NewsWatch.

FACTS.com

Safe Drinking Water Act signed. (1996, August 22). <u>Facts on File World News Digest</u>. Retrieved January 16, 2003, from FACTS.com.

Health and Wellness Resource Center

(sample citation for an article from a reference **book**)

Jacobs, J.T. (2001). Prevention of sexually transmitted diseases. In <u>Clinical reference Systems</u>. Broomfield, CO: McKesson HBOC. Retrieved January 16, 2003, from Health and Wellness Resource Center.

(sample citation for a **journal article**)

Parker, R.A. (2002). A 45-year old woman with obsessive-compulsive disorder: One Year later. <u>JAMA</u>, 287(8), 1037. Retrieved January 16, 2003, from Health and Wellness Resource Center.

ProQuest (sample citation for a **newspaper article**)

Stevenson, R.W. (2003, January 15). Bush urges Congress to extend welfare law, with Changes. <u>New York Times</u>, p. A18 (Late Edition, East Coast). Retrieved January 16, 2003, from ProQuest.

Sources: Publication Manual of the American Psychological Association, Fifth Ed. And APAStyle.org:
Electronic References
<u>*http://www.apastyle.org/elecmedia.html*</u>
Prepared by T. Stough & H. Rodriguez, Fall 2003 OCLIB

76   How Do I Evaluate Web Pages?

Authority

- Is it clear who is sponsoring the creation and maintenance of the page?
- Is there information available describing the purpose of the sponsoring organization?
- Is there a way of verifying the legitimacy of the page's sponsor? For instance, is a phone number or address available to contact for more information?
- Is it clear who developed and wrote the material? Are his/her qualifications for writing on this topic clearly stated? Is there contact information for the author of the material?

Accuracy

- Are the sources for factual information given so they can be verified?
- Is it clear who has the responsibility for the accuracy of the information presented?
- If statistical data is presented in graphs or charts, are they labeled clearly?

Objectivity

- Is the page and the information included provided as a public service?
- Is it free of advertising?
- If there is advertising on the page, is it clearly separated from the informational content?
- Are there any other signs of bias?

Currency

- Are there dates on the page to indicate the following:
    a. When the page was written?
    b. When the page was first placed online?
    c. When the page was last revised or edited?
- Are there any other indications that the material is updated frequently to ensure currency of the data?
- Are the links on the page up-to-date?

Coverage

- If there is a print equivalent to the Web page, is there clear indication of whether the entire work or only a portion of it is available on the Web?
- If the material is from a work that is out of copyright (as is often the case with a dictionary or thesaurus), has there been an effort to update the material to make it more current?
- Is there any other evidence of omissions?
- Does it cover the subject adequately?

Based on the following WWW page: Alexander, J. & Tate, M. (1996, August 8). Teaching Critical Evaluation Skills for World Wide Web Resources. Retrieved on September 25, 2000.

77 How Can I Use the College Library More Effectively?

The library is the major student resource on any college campus. The effective use of your college library will provide you with valuable information in completing many of your research/writing assignments. To use the library more effectively, familiarize yourself with the features of the library. Take a walking tour of the library. During the walking tour, identify maps and newspapers. Most libraries have handouts and brochures which describe the services offered to students. Talk to the librarian to learn more about the library. Identify the location of the circulation section and the reference section. Ask the librarian about databases available to students. Databases are proprietary which means your library pays for their use and consequently their use may have restrictions. Accessing information will involve the use of your student identification and PIN number. Since the library is your most valuable resource, be sure learn to use it well.

78 How Do I Conduct an Information Search?

One of the most important activities conducted by any college student is the search for information. The most important factor in conducting an information search is to have a clear idea of what you are looking for. When beginning your search, it is important to formulate the right question to ask to lead you to the information you seek. When you begin your information search, have a copy of your assignment. If you are using the information search to do a paper, how long does the paper have to be?

Many information searches begin with a computer search. Most students rely heavily on databases. There are many advantages to using the Internet but there are also disadvantages. Most important is the credibility of your reference. The Internet may give you specific information but may not give you a broad perspective on the issue your investigating. Some instructors require that you use books for references and will limit the use of Internet resources. Remember, the search for information should be careful, thoughtful, comprehensive, and in-depth.

169

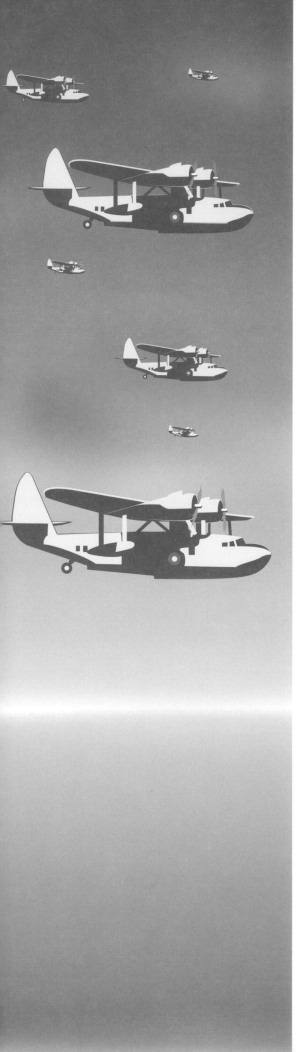

 # How Do I Make Sense of the Information?

The more you know about your topic the easier it will be to make sense of the information you have collected. In making sense of researched information, it is especially important to pay attention to your sources. What makes your sources credible? Information you are using should stand the test of a critical analysis. Look for facts, causal relationships, correlations, and evidence of support for premises and suppositions. What are the major theses in your sources of information? Is the information presented in a logical fashion? Making sense of information usually involves sorting, observing, selecting, classifying, and analyzing information.

Life
Management
Skills

How Do I Set Goals?

Goals give purpose and meaning to life. Goals establish direction by helping us set our course. The pursuit of goals can be a source of joy and excitement. The process of working toward goals enriches our lives and fills the emptiness that many of us experience. Goals help eliminate confusion and doubt about what we should be doing with our lives. An aimless and wandering life can generate much unhappiness and disillusionment. Goals are desired outcomes, results, things we want to achieve; conditions we want to create and things we want. Goals are written statements of intention.

Goals as Organizers

Goals are the organizers of our lives. By setting goals we design our lives. Consciously setting goals can be a difficult endeavor. Ideally, the goals we set come through careful consideration of what we want. When goals come from others, and we do not clearly own our goals, we are headed for difficulty. Many of us lack a clear idea of what we want out of life. Discovering what we want emanates from a process of achieving self-knowledge. Self-knowledge is the foundation of goal setting. Clarity about what we want out of life and the goals we have set frequently put us in conflict with others because they may not want for us what we want for ourselves. Thinking for ourselves is an important part of goal setting.

Risking Failure and Rejection

Reaching for our goals frequently involves the possibility of failure. If we are to achieve our goals, we may also have to risk rejection. An important aspect of goal attainment is persistence in the face of failure. Believing in ourselves and understanding that many things are achievable over time if we persist serves to strengthen our confidence. If we do not risk failure and rejection, we may settle for the familiar and comfortable. We must go beyond self-imposed limitations to achieve. Goal setting involves reaching beyond our perceived limitations. In setting goals, we stretch and reach beyond the familiar. Much is possible if we are willing to risk.

Discovery of Wants

As we begin to discover what we want from life, we can begin to formulate goals based on those desires. Formulating goals involves writing and stating goals. After we have written and stated our goals, we devise plans to achieve our goals. A goal setting plan is stated in specific steps to reach our goals.

Goals and Objectives

A goal requires specific steps leading to a desired outcome. The steps taken to achieve that outcome are called objectives. Objectives are the work, the activities, the stages we go through to achieve our goals. The more specific and concrete the objectives, the easier it is to evaluate the progress toward the completion of goals. A system of evaluating progress toward goals is desirable because it gives us information we may need to redirect our efforts, and it lets us know whether we are on course.

Make a list of the three things you want most. Transform this list into goal statements. Make a list of objectives leading to the achievement of each goal.

 ## Which Communication Skills Are Applicable to Everyday Life?

Communication consists of verbal and nonverbal messages which are expressed within the context of behavioral, emotional, and cognitive processes. Learning about communication involves learning how people exchange ideas in real life situations and learning how we communicate in addressing real life issues. Communication has many dimensions. We learn to communicate more effectively by examining how we communicate. Communication skills are vital since they are used in every aspect of our lives.

Communication Skills

Listening

Effective listening requires effort. Listening is much more than parroting back the words we have heard someone express. Listening involves being fully available and present for others. It is through listening that we come to know others

"Own" Your Communication and Perceptions, and Avoid Speaking for Others

When we "own" our communication, we make it clear that we speak for ourselves and no one else. Pronouns such as I, me, my, mine, show ownership of communication. This is sometimes called sending "I messages." By owning our communication and perceptions, we give others room to own their communication and perceptions. Owning communication creates clarity and allows for the acceptance of personal responsibility.

Take Responsibility for Your Thoughts, Feelings, and Reactions

When I take responsibility for my thoughts, feelings, and reactions, I do not blame you for how I think, feel, and act. The quality of my experience is my responsibility. My happiness and satisfaction are my responsibility, and you are not responsible for creating these experiences for me.

Trust

Trust is essential for effective communication. Without trust, communication breaks down. Trust is difficult to define, and the dynamics of trust are complex. Trust is usually based on agreed-upon conditions and expectations about behavior. Violations of these agreements frequently destroy the trust and the relationship.

Be Open and Honest

By being open and honest, we develop authentic relationships. Openness and honesty form the basis for mutual understanding and the development of intimacy. Deception, hiding, and lying greatly interfere with the quality of communication.

Be "For Real" (Congruent)

When I am congruent, I say what I mean, and I mean what I say. Congruence means that there is a consistency between what I appear to be and what I actually am. Feelings and actions go together.

Take Risks

It is always risky to be open and honest with others. When we share our honest thoughts and feelings, there is always a potential for conflict. However, without risking conflict, we lose out on opportunities for intimacy and growth.

Be Cautious When Trying to Figure Others Out

Many people resent efforts to analyze and figure them out. This tends to result in a person feeling treated as a thing rather than as a person. Usually, people want to be cared for, supported and accepted, not "figured out." When we attempt to figure others out, we put ourselves in the position of being one up on the other person. We frequently assume that we know more about the other person than that person knows about him/herself. Figuring others out is best left to psychotherapists.

Get in Touch with Your Thoughts, Feelings, and Reactions

Many of us struggle with being in touch with our feelings. This creates significant barriers in communication. How we think greatly determines how we feel, and how we feel significantly affects how we act. By being in touch with our thoughts, feelings and reactions, we can better express and communicate to others our inner life.

Attend to Verbal and Non-Verbal Cues

In communicating effectively we need to attend to both verbal and non-verbal cues presented by the other. The non-verbal communication is analogous to music which forms the background for the lyrics of a song. We need to listen to the music as others communicate to us. The non-verbal cues frequently contain the message. Ask yourself, "Am I getting the non-verbal message?" or "Have I listened to the music?"

Paraphrase Others' Communication

When we paraphrase, or restate, what others are saying, we demonstrate that we are paying attention, listening, and are concerned. Paraphrasing allows us to check on the messages that are being conveyed to us. Paraphrasing helps us understand the meaning of an expression. Paraphrasing demonstrates an intent to understand.

Be Cautious When Offering Solutions to the Problems of Others

It is usually best for people to come to their own solutions to problems. Offering solutions undermines the responsibility of others to direct their own lives. We frequently make the mistake of offering simple solutions to long term problems. Individuals are usually not committed to the solutions of problems that come from others. Solutions offered to others establish an unequal relationship. This frequently interferes with communication.

Maintain a Non–Judgmental Attitude

No one likes to feel judged by others. Nothing will cause a breakdown of communication more quickly than a person believing s/he is being judged. In many situations a non-judgmental attitude is required. We must be cautious of imposing our belief system on others which usually is the basis for judging others. Judgment of right and wrong greatly increases the defensiveness of others. Openness and flexibility through a non-judgmental attitude facilitates communication. Our moral system should not be imposed on others.

Accept Differences

We need to recognize the right of individuals to be different. Differences allow for diversity and make life more interesting. We can learn to accept differences by understanding the threat that the differences pose to us. The more clarity we have about who we are, the less threatening differences become to us.

Develop Empathic Responses

The cornerstone of effective communication is the ability to see the world through the eyes of others. Understanding the world from your viewpoint and being sensitive to that viewpoint greatly enhances communication. Being empathic requires careful listening, imagination, and the suspension of our own world view. We respond empathically when we accurately capture the nature of the experience of other people. Empathy forms the basis for love and compassion. Without empathy, there is no compassion.

How Can I Communicate My Feelings to Others?

Getting in Touch with Feelings

Feelings and emotions are an important part of who you are. We are not always in touch with our feelings. Getting in touch with our feelings requires paying attention to our body and mind. Awareness of our internal reactions helps us get in touch with feelings. In order to express our feelings, we need to start by getting in touch with them.

Awareness of Feelings

Sometimes we are not even aware of what we feel. But if you are not aware of a feeling, how can you express it? Awareness of feelings is absolutely critical. Not to be aware of feelings is not to be aware of yourself. It takes practice to be aware of how you feel, because most of us habitually do not pay attention to our feelings. You need to change that habit and become accustomed to paying attention to your feelings. A learned pattern of "tuning in" to internal stimuli will heighten your self-awareness and thus increase your awareness of feelings.

Describing Feelings

Feelings may be difficult to express because of linguistic limitations. Just as awareness of feelings requires attention and practice, we also need to practice describing feelings. If I cannot describe how I feel, how can you possibly understand my feelings? It is through the description of feelings that we communicate feelings. It is through the labeling of feelings that we communicate feelings.

Labeling Feelings

It is important to be concise in our communication about feelings. We need to make concise statements about how we feel instead of giving elaborate explanations that may be confusing. For example, saying, "I feel sad" is clear and unambiguous, whereas a long explanation may be confusing and hard to follow. A concise statement which incorporates a feeling word facilitates feeling communication. Examples of feeling words are: angry, hurt, sad, lonely, depressed, lost, worried, happy, joyful, excited, and elated.

Expression of Feelings

We tend to be indirect when we communicate our feelings because it is often frightening to communicate feelings directly. I do not know how you are going to respond to my feelings; therefore, I avoid communicating feelings to you directly. Fear of expressing feelings is probably the greatest obstacle to the expression of feelings.

How Do I Balance School, Work, and Family Commitments?

Many community college students are faced with the dilemma of balancing school, work, and family. A key to balancing your commitments is time management. You need to decide how much time you are able to spend on each commitment. After you've examined your time allocation, you need to consider your goals. How important are your goals and are you willing to sacrifice to achieve your goals?

For example, if you are married and have children, how will you provide for your family when you are attending class and studying? Everyone in your family may have to make sacrifices to help you achieve your goals. In addition, if you work full time, you will find it very difficult to maintain a full load. However, many students have supportive employers and can maintain a flexible work schedule. The conflict between school, family, and work need not prevent you from achieving your goals. Goals are attained in small step. Don't be deterred by taking longer to achieve your goals. Significant goals are achieved through sustained effort. Your education will not only benefit you, it will benefit everyone around you.

84 How Can I Manage Stress?

All of us experience daily stress; some of us may experience daily distress. Distress is more injurious than stress. Distress occurs when coping capacities are being taxed to the limit. The result is were and tear on the body. Stress is a reaction to demands made on the body to adapt and change. Rapidity of change, daily hassles, and a hurried lifestyle all contribute to the stress and strain of living.

Appraisal of Stress

The impact of stress is largely determined by the interpretations of stressful events. The mental appraisal you make may be the single most important factor in determining the impact of stress.

Change and Stress

Life holds many changes which lead to stress. It is a good idea to decrease the rate of change. Researchers have determined that the more changes you have experienced in a year's time, the greater the likelihood you will get sick. The rapidity of change, frequency of change, and intensity of change are major sources of stress for people. A hurried lifestyle may be a sign of being under stress. This is another factor to consider in assessing your lifestyle.

Stress Reduction

Stress reduction begins with an assessment of lifestyle. Mechanisms to reduce stress need to be incorporated into our daily lives. Sleep, nutrition, and exercise form the foundation of a good stress reduction program. The quality of sleep, proper nutrition, and appropriate exercise contribute significantly to the quality of life. We need a place to remove ourselves from daily stresses. We need a place to rejuvenate and regenerate. We need a place to be alone and to be quiet.

Relaxation and Stress

One of the biggest problems in learning how to relax and relieve stress is that we do not know the difference between states of tension and relaxation. Sometimes we feel relaxed, but in reality we are not. We must learn to discriminate between states of tension and stress as opposed to states of deep relaxation.

Progressive Relaxation

A very simple technique used by many psychologists to help people relax is to tighten and contract muscles followed by relaxing those muscles, and then feeling and sensing the difference. Make a tight fist for six seconds and pay attention the way your muscles feel. Relax the tight fist and sense the difference between tight, tense muscles and relaxed muscles. You can do this with all muscles groups, you are using the technique known as progressive relaxation.

There are many ways to alleviate and protect yourself from distress. An excellent option when you are confused about stress or distress is to pursue psychotherapy.

85 How Do I Overcome Procrastination?

The following strategy has been formulated to help you overcome procrastination. For many, procrastination is a deeply entrenched problem. Your level of motivation or desire to overcome this problem will significantly influence the success of your efforts. Understanding the root cause of your procrastination will also significantly influence your ability to overcome this problem.

Admit

As most people will agree, admitting that you have a problem is a preliminary step to overcoming the problem. Failure to recognize that you have a problem makes it virtually impossible to solve the problem.

Analyze

Analyze the causes of your procrastination problem. There are apparent and non-apparent reasons for procrastination. The greater the procrastination problem, the more likely that non-apparent reasons are behind the problem.

Monitor

You determine the size of a problem by monitoring and measuring the problem. You can count the number of times you procrastinate doing important tasks on a daily, weekly, and monthly basis. Choose a system to count the number of times you procrastinate doing important tasks on a daily basis. Monitor this behavior for about two weeks. Determine the frequency of your procrastination.

Realize

Think about the short and long range consequences of postponing important activities. Be conscious of those consequences. Realizing the consequences of postponing important activities may deter procrastination. Knowing the consequences of your behavior helps you stay on target.

Remind

Remind yourself of the long-term benefits of accomplishing important tasks. Reminding ourselves of the long-term benefits of completing important tasks encourage us to complete the tasks. The more often we complete those tasks, the better we feel about ourselves.

Know

Know what you are going to accomplish specifically and what the benefits will be.

Plan

Plan for gradual change. Do not expect to overcome the problem with procrastination overnight. Overcoming procrastination is a constant struggle and challenge. Look for opportunities not to procrastinate. Without a plan procrastination is nearly impossible to overcome.

How Can I Make More Effective Decisions?

Decision-making is a vital part of personal growth and development. It involves taking control of one's life, nurturing self-esteem, and having a sense of empowerment. Decisions shape and form our lives. Choosing is life's defining factor. We are our decisions. By actively choosing, we take control of our lives. Making our own decisions solidifies our independence and autonomy. When we choose for ourselves, we are responsible for ourselves. By making our own decisions, we separate ourselves from others. Through decisions, we reveal who we are and for what we stand. Our decisions define the content of our character.

Students make many life decisions, such as which relationships to cultivate and maintain, which institutions to attend, and other career and lifestyle choices. These life decisions cause a great deal of stress because they have a long-term impact on the life of the individual. Understanding the decision-making process eases the accompanying stress and conflict. Decision-making is a process of many discrete problems, generating alternatives, selecting an alternative, and implementing the decision. Decision-making involves bringing about desirable situations, conditions, circumstances, events, and personal states of satisfaction.

The Decision–Making Process

Step 1. Identifying, defining, sorting, and analyzing issues, problems, and concerns which require a decision

Step 2. Gathering information which sheds light on the issues, problems, and concerns which are being addressed

Step 3. Generating courses of action and alternatives

Step 4. Exploring feelings about actions and alternatives

Step 5. Weighing alternatives

Step 6. Predicting outcomes and consequences

Step 7. Making the decision

Step 8. Implementing the decision

Step 9. Evaluating the decision

Step 10. Making new decisions

Creating
a
Vision

## CHAPTER 7

# How Do I Create a Vision for My Life?

A vision stirs us into action. It provides a framework for our existence. A vision consists of mental pictures about past, present, and future. It is our mental plan for our life's direction. We can describe and articulate our vision to ourselves and to others. It contains the range of possibilities available to us to actualize our potentialities.

Power of Vision

A vision is both a conscious and unconscious construction. A vision is what you want it to be. It's what you see for yourself. A vision gives strength, meaning, purpose, and personal power. It directs and focuses our energies. A vision is an expression of our values, goals, and purpose, and frequently contains a self-transcending aspect, a belief in something greater than ourselves. For many, a vision is an anchor which holds us steady through life's turmoil and disappointments. A vision provides hope in times of despair.

Vision-Makers

We are vision-makers and can create a positive vision for our lives. A positive vision creates hope and many possibilities for the future. Have you actively created your vision? Have you created your vision by default? If you need to re-create your vision, you may want to start by examining your values and dreams and determine what gives your life purpose and meaning.

Importance of Vision

A vision is important because it gives us a sense of where we have been, where we are now, and where we are going. A vision can help us overcome a profound sense of emptiness and loneliness. A vision gives us a sense of safety and security. A vision gives our lives purpose. A vision gives us a reason to live.

88 What Is the Career Development Process?

Self–Assessment

A comprehensive process of self-exploration, self discovery, self-examination, and self-evaluation comprises the self-assessment process. We explore needs, wants, preferences, and past experience, including both work and school. We may discover additional assets and find new sources of strength. We examine values, interests, and skills, and we discover our purpose. Our purpose forms a framework for our life's vision and reflects our passion. We use journals, interest and value inventories, personality type indicators, and computerized career planning systems to augment our self-assessment. We synthesize and evaluate the results of this process in order to make career decisions.

Career Search

A career search leads us to the college library and career center. We use the results of our self-assessment to narrow our search. We look for careers that match our values, needs, wants, preferences, and vision for our lives. We use standard publications such as *The Dictionary of Occupational Titles* and *The Occupational Outlook Handbook* to conduct our search. Our career search may include networking with others to find career opportunities.

Job Hunt

A job hunt leads us to a job or series of jobs which ultimately lead us to a career. A job hunt includes traditional and non-traditional strategies for obtaining a job. We usually find a job through people we know. Making contact with others is essential to effective job hunting. A job hunt frequently involves finding the person with the power to hire within the organization in which you are seeking employment. The ability to market yourself is essential to effective job hunting and job attainment.

How Do I Match My Personality with a Career?

Thousands of careers and jobs have been identified and placed into career and occupational categories. This categorical approach makes choosing a career significantly more manageable. One aspect of career planning involves matching your personality type to an occupational environment.

According to John Holland in *Making Vocational Choices: A Theory of Careers*, people can be divided into six personality and occupational environment types. They include Realistic, Investigative, Artistic, Social, Enterprising, and Conventional.

Realistic people are robust, practical, and strong. They work in skilled trades or technical jobs.

Investigative people are scientific, task-oriented, shy, and introspective. They work in scientific and laboratory jobs.

Artistic people are creative, and expressive. They work in jobs that involve words, music, or art.

Social people are humanistic, responsible, and sociable. They work with people in healing, teaching, and helping.

Enterprising people are driven, dominating, and enjoy leading others. They work in sales, merchandising, and politics.

Conventional people are conforming systemic, and well structured. They work in office jobs and organizations.

This personality-occupational system is designed to help you match your personality type with a career category.

90 What References Will Help Me Find a Job and Develop a Career?

Library Books

The Best Jobs for the 21st Century
HF5382.K68

Complete Guide to International Jobs and Careers
HF5549.5E45 K73

Dictionary of Occupational Titles
REF HB2595 .U543

Discover the Best Jobs for You!: Find the Job to Get a Life You Love
HF 5382.K69

Earth Work: Resource Guide to Nationwide Green Jobs
REF GE60.E27

The Encyclopedia of Careers and Vocational Guidance
REF HF5381.E52

Occupational Outlook Handbook
REF HF5381.A10362

Web Sites

America's Career InfoNet
http://www.acinet.org/acinet/default.asp

California Occupational Guides
http://www.calmis.cahwnet.gov/htmlfile/subject/guide.htm

Flipdog.com
http://www.flipdog.com/

IMDiversity.com Career Center
http://www.imdiversity.com/

Job Board for Hispanic & Bilingual Professionals
http://www.latpro.com

Monster.com
http://www.monster.com/

Occupational Outlook Handbook Online
http://www.bls.gov/oco/home.htm

Glossary of Academic Terms

academic advisement   interactive process of shared responsibility between advisor and student focusing on helping students reach goals by selecting, deciding, and succeeding in courses and programs

academic probation   grade point average is considered to be academically below satisfactory progress

academic renewal   process by which a student may petition the college to eliminate previous substandard work

admissions and records   office and staff that admits and registers students in classes

articulation process   developing a formal, written and published agreement that identifies courses (or sequences of courses) from a sending institution that are comparable to, or acceptable in lieu of, specific course requirements at a "receiving" institution (four-year university or another community college)

assessment process   testing students to determine levels of proficiency in selected skills and subjects for the purpose of appropriate level course placement

Associate in Arts/Associate in Science Degrees (A.A. or A.S.)   degrees granted by community colleges upon completion of required courses, units, and competencies

Certificate of Achievement   certificate granted by a community college which recognizes a student's satisfactory completion of an occupational program

certification   official process by which the community college will verify to four-year colleges/universities that a student has completed all or part of the lower division general education requirements for that institution

closed classes   classes which reach the predetermined maximum of enrolled students

college catalog   college publication describing courses, academic programs, student services, general regulations, requirements and procedures

community college   a two-year college offering a wide range of programs which lead to Associate Degrees

counseling   interactive process of shared responsibility which helps students resolve conflicts and reach goals

course   subject area of instruction

course title   phrase descriptive of the course content

credit   successful completion of a course, usually expressed in the number of units of course work

credit by examination   course credits or units granted to a student through an examination process

credit/no credit ("CR/NR")   grading option in which the student is given a grade of "CR" (Credit) or "NC" (No Credit) rather than a letter grade of "A", "B:, "C", "D", or "F"

curriculum   instructional program of a college

discipline   an organized area of study

dismissal/disqualification   dismissal from college based on substandard academic progress

educational program   planned sequence of courses leading to a goal such as a Certificate of Achievement or an Associate Degree

electives   courses that are not required subjects but are taken based on individual choice

enrollment   part of the registration process in which the student is placed in class

general education requirements   specific group of course requirements that must be met in order to obtain a degree

grade points   numerical value of a college letter grade (A=4, B=3, C=2, D=1, and F=0) multiplied by the number of units of a specific course

impacted (over subscribed) program majors or programs in which student applicants exceed available spaces

incomplete ("I")   letter "I" is recorded on the student's permanent record when the student is not able to complete a course due to circumstances beyond his/her control

intercollegiate   between or among colleges, such as in competitive sports events

lower division   the first two years of college

major   a planned series of required courses in the student's main area of study

matriculation   process a student goes through to get ready to register for classes: includes completion of an application, assessment, orientation, and a counseling appointment

non-penalty drop period   beginning period of regular semester during which a student can drop a class without notations on records

placement tests   tests given prior to registration to determine the most appropriate class level

prerequisite   requirement that must be satisfied before enrolling in a particular course

probation   academic standing which indicates substantial academic performance

transfer   transition of a student from a community college to a four-year college/ university

transfer courses   courses designated as baccalaureate level and articulated to four-year institutions

units   amount of college credit earned by completing a course during a semester

withdrawal   leaving a class by filing appropriate forms within a specified time frame

193

REFERENCES

Catalogs

2000-2001 Catalog
Amarillo College
Amarillo, Texas 79178

2000-2002 Catalog
Blue Mountain Community College
Pendleton, Oregon 97801

2002-2003 Catalog
Brookhaven College
Farmers Branch, Texas 75244

2000-2001 Catalog
Broward Community College
Fort Lauderdale, Florida 33301

2000-2002 Catalog
Cayuga Community College
Fulton, New York 13069

2000-2001 Catalog
Central Oregon Community College
Bend, Oregon 97701

2000-2001 Catalog
Chemeketa Community College
Salem, Oregon 97309

2002-2003 Catalog
Coastal Bend College
Beeville, Texas 78102

2003-2004 Catalog
College of Lake County
Grayslake, Illinois 60030

2003-2004 Catalog
Delgado Community College
New Orleans, Louisiana 70114

2000-2001 Catalog
Eastfield College
Mesquite, Texas 75150

2000-2002 Catalog
Edmonds Community College
Lynnwood, Washington 98036

2000-2002 Catalog
Finger Lakes Community College
Canandaigua, New York 14424

2000-2001 Catalog
Florida Community College
Jacksonville, Florida 32205

1999-2001 Catalog
Illinois Valley Community College
Oglesby, Illinois 61348

2000-2002 Catalog
Joliet Junior College
Joliet, Illinois 60431

2000-2001 Catalog
Lewis and Clark Community College
Godfrey, Illinois 62035

2003-2004 Catalog
Oakton Community College
Des Plaines, Illinois 60016

2003-2004 Catalog
Oxnard College
Oxnard, California 93033

2000-2001 Catalog
Palm Beach Community College
Palm Beach Gardens, Florida 33410

2001-2003 Catalog
Palo Verde College
Blythe, California 92225

2000-2001 Catalog
Santa Fe Community College
Gainesville, Florida 32606

2001-2003 Catalog
Sullivan County Community College
Loch Sheldrake, New York 12759

2000-2001 Catalog
Treasure Valley Community College
Ontario, Oregon 97914

2003-2004 Catalog
Ventura College
Ventura, California 93003

1999-2001 Catalog
Whatcom Community College
Bellingham, Washington 98226

Schedule of Classes

Spring 2004
Austin Community College
Austin, Texas 78752

Spring 2004
Black Hawk College
Moline, Illinois 61265

Fall-Spring 2003-2004
Brazosport College
Lake Jackson, Texas 77566

Fall 2003
College of the Sequoias
Visalia, California 93277

Spring 2003
Cuyamaca College
El Cajon, California 92019

Fall 2003
Delgado Community College
New Orleans, Louisiana 70119

Fall 2003
El Paso Community College
Decatur, Georgia 30033

Spring 2004
Lee College
Baytown, Texas 77522

Spring 2003
Miramar College
San Diego, California 92108

Spring 2004
Moraine Valley Community College
Palos Hills, Illinois 60465

Spring 2004
Morton College
Cicero, Illinois 60804

Fall 2003
Mount San Antonio College
Walnut, California 91789

Spring 2004
Oakton Community College
Des Plains, Illinois 60016

Summer and Fall 2003
Palo Alto College
San Antonio, Texas 78224

Fall 2003
Rio Hondo College
Whittier, California 90601

Spring 2003
Southwestern College
Chula Vista, California 91910

Fall 2003
The Peralta Colleges
Oakland, California 94606

Fall-Spring-Summer 2003-2004
The Victoria College
Victoria, Texas 77901

Spring 2004
Triton College
River Grove, Illinois 60171

Spring 2004
Tyler Junior College
Tyler, Texas 75701

Other Sources of Information

College Orientation Brochures

The Empowered Student by Anthony Raptis

Telephone Surveys and Interviews

ERIC Website – http://www.gseis.ucla.edu/ERIC/fag.html

Websites

Index